Shine!
Healthcare
Leadership Distilled

Shine!
Healthcare Leadership Distilled

INCREASE YOUR BOTTOM-LINE THROUGH
IMPROVED LEADERSHIP

Matthew J. Hess MBA, MA, SPHR

authorHOUSE®

AuthorHouse™
1663 Liberty Drive
Bloomington, IN 47403
www.authorhouse.com
Phone: 1-800-839-8640

Published by AuthorHouse   11/07/2012

ISBN: 978-1-4772-8574-9 (sc)
ISBN: 978-1-4772-8573-2 (e)

Library of Congress Control Number: 2012920421

CONTENTS

Chapter 6
Ethics and Recognition
An ethical culture does not accidentally happen.

Element of Leadership # 6— *"Recognize employees for behaviors you want to encourage."*

page 86

—wwo~o⊙ro⊙ro⊙o~w—

Chapter 7
Employment Law and Interviewing Effectively
Make the right hiring decisions so you can focus on staffing fluidity and teamwork. Take time at the beginning of the employment relationship to ensure you have the right person for the long term.

Element of Leadership # 7— *"Hire hard so you can manage easy."*

page 108

—wwo~o⊙ro⊙ro⊙o~w—

Chapter 8
Documentation, Investigations, Discipline and Appraisals
Objectivity and non-bias are critical to gain trust and respect from employees.

Element of Leadership # 8— *"A coin has two sides, but the value is in the middle."*

page 123

—wwo~o⊙ro⊙ro⊙o~w—

Author's Foreword

Shine! was developed from my belief that people want to be as good as they can be at whatever it is they do. People, given the right information, knowledge and skills will flourish. We all want to be great at something. Why not our world of work?

Often employees are thrust into leadership positions which require management, organization, communication skills, and a general understanding of the world of interpersonal leadership. Too often in healthcare great people are promoted to their own level of incompetence. They are good, long-term employees; they get along with everyone and follow policy. These are great qualities in an employee; however, they are only a small component to outstanding leadership. In fact, we promote employees and they too often fail or struggle more than they have to. Administration looks around and asks, "What the heck is going on? She was such a great employee before we promoted her."

It is no different than asking the Director of HR to start IV's. People would say, "My gosh, he sure has a lot of vein bleeds." The Director of HR would ask, "Vein bleed, what's a vein bleed?" Simply put, no one stopped to say to the Director of HR, "Hey, there are a few things you may need to know about this whole starting IV's thing." That's what we do to people when we thrust them into a leadership role with no training. We set them and the people around them up for failure. We all know why employees most often leave employment—their direct supervisor. I believe leaders are made, not born. The equation is simple.

Improved leadership → improved employee satisfaction → improved patient satisfaction → increased bottom line

Leading people is about understanding what people do, how they do it, and most importantly why they do it. Shine! is the confluence of ten years' experience as a Director of HR in Healthcare, twelve years in higher education; teaching a variety of business and human resource courses, and currently adjunct faculty at Concord University's School of Business, as well as earning a B.A. in psychology, a Master of Arts in HR, a MBA and a Senior Professional in Human Resources (SPHR), certification.

Shine's! goal is to create better leaders so the employees that work for them can find satisfaction which, as we know, leads to patient satisfaction, and drives turnover down. Fluency in the department and organization will result in less turnover which leads to cut training, overtime and orientation costs. It is estimated that one employee turnover can cost an employer from $30,000 to as much as $60,000. Most importantly however, employee satisfaction and patient satisfaction will increase with well-versed managers who speak the same language and can use each other as resources. Shine! is the product of working with employees and leaders and learning in which areas they need the most education and a deeper understanding. I want to prepare employees to become leaders, and to help current leaders become better so the care they provide will improve and patient satisfaction will increase. It's the right thing to do for the patient and the bottom line especially with CMS reimbursement and Obamacare pending and in full enforcement.

Shine! is a finely tuned distillation that culminates in the Eight Elements of Leadership. It is a simple approach that has removed the superfluous aspects of business school and practice and left the most valuable information in a form that builds on itself with each chapter. There is one key idea from each chapter and these are the Eight Elements of Leadership. Shine! is intended to help leaders understand themselves and find their full potential, while teaching leaders to help others find theirs. We all want to Shine!—the leader, employee, patient, and bottom line.

We, as leaders want people to find their self-actualization so they thrive, are satisfied, engaged and constantly looking for ways to improve, not just get through a shift. Each of the Eight Elements of Leadership is elaborated on within its respective chapter. People spend too much time at work to just get by, when what they really want to do is Shine!

Chapter 1—Diversity and the Changing Management Paradigm

A Brief History

A changing work environment is inevitable. Often the greatest factor affecting the work environment is the actual workforce and how they view their worlds. Consequently, the largest variable that leaders face in a changing business climate is how they adapt to these changing perspectives. First, is a leader able to see and understand the changes in the environment? Are they able to see the changes in people as simply different, rather than inferior or superior? Second, can a leader apply what they've learned and adapt to these changes?

The most important aspect to seeing these changes objectively is to understand what the changes are, how they happened and why they occurred. Often there are barriers between one generation and the next. Each generation builds their viewpoints based on different experiences in time. Because our experiences are so different, it isn't uncommon for each new generation to view the up and coming generation negatively without considering that different isn't always worse, it is just different. Below are common criticisms of Baby Boomers regarding Generation X.

> "I don't know what's wrong with this generation, whatever you call it, Gen X, Gen X games, whatever. Their work ethic is terrible and they don't care. They're job hoppers and they're only concerned with themselves."

It even goes back to the WWII generation, (The Traditional Generation) that gave birth to the baby boomers.

> *"They're out of control, radicals, all they want to do is drugs*
> *and have sex with anything that moves. Where's the modesty?*
> *You can't get them to do any work.*
> *My gosh they stink, and that hair."*

Now, even today, we still hear the same sentiments being echoed by Generation X, about Generation Y.

> *"Generation Y, why is the question, why are they so lazy, and*
> *why aren't they loyal? Why don't they care about anything?*
> *Why can't they work as hard as me? They don't want to do*
> *anything except play video games and text message, why? Why*
> *do they feel so entitled? It's ridiculous."*

It's as if each generation can't stop to remember how they were viewed and how they were treated, because with each new generation the same treatment they didn't like is passed on to the up and coming generation. The key to remember is that the new generation is responding to the old generation and, most often, the things they didn't like about it. As Jack White says, "You can't take the effect and make it the cause."

There is a theme from generation to generation. It is that the generation in power is right and the generation who wants power is wrong and therefore must be subjugated for the continued power of the older generation. It's a perpetual cycle that can only be broken through understanding and adaptability. Remember, one size does not fit all.

> *"Diversity is the spark of innovation and creativity."*

There are very clear reasons as to why these generations see the world of work differently; self-esteem, involvement, teams, empowerment and most importantly, a desire to balance work-life with their family and personal lives. The need for employees to look out for their own best interests and feel satisfied in their work life has become paramount in the business world. Generation X threw the ally-oop and Generation Y is taking this idea and slamming it home for the dunk. We can all learn from each other.

The Changing Social Contract

> *"The* **social contract** *of the past was an implicit understanding between employers and employees that hard work and loyalty would result in continued employment. This was prevalent in prior years. However, it does seem to be true that for a growing number of organizations, they cannot maintain this contract. The assumption that hard work and loyalty from employees will be matched by the job security provided by the employer is no longer as valid as it once was." (French, 51)*

Why the Social Contract Has Changed

Globalization or the breaking down of trade barriers between countries started social contract changes. It became easier to do business in other countries. Because of globalization, **outsourcing** or moving operations to foreign nations increased and many companies took their manufacturing out of the U.S. due to lower wages. This left the U.S. economy stagnant and with a loss of good, strong, blue-collar jobs. The manufacturing sector was outsourced. As a result, labor jobs moved to places like China and an increase for technology and service workers occurred in the U.S. with the aging Baby Boomer population.

The problem for many years was that the educational level of the U.S. wasn't at the level needed to perform the knowledge jobs that slowly replaced labor jobs. The shift from **labor jobs to knowledge jobs** occurred quicker than the U.S. could react due to the mass outsourcing. Unemployment was the result which lent itself to the reeducation of the U.S. Finally, with an increasingly educated nation, often in service oriented jobs such as nursing and healthcare, the expectations of what work meant, changed.

Generational leadership changes are constantly happening as well; out with the old and in with the new. It is a constant cycle that perplexes each new generation as they fight for influence and control. Currently, we are experiencing a shift as Baby Boomers exit the workforce and Generation X replaces them in management roles.

With this, Generation Y is stepping into the roles that Generation X is vacating.

However, all of this stair stepping has been stagnated due to poor stock market performance, and retirements being postponed. Baby-Boomers are staying in the workforce longer than they had planned which has caused Generation X to stay lower on the workforce totem for longer which ultimately doesn't open new positions for Generation Y. Because of this and many other reasons we'll discover later, the various generations view the world differently.

Generational Characteristics

"1946-1964"	"1965-1980"	"1981-forward"
80 Million	**44-50 Million**	**70 Million**
Baby Boomers	**Generation X**	**Generation Y**
Fair day's work	Accountability,	Tech Savvy,
for a fair day's pay.	Teamwork,	Family Centric,
Loyal, Hard Working,	Innovation,	Confident/Ambitious,
Security, Low Risk	Participation,	Achievement Oriented,
Don't Question Authority	Empowerment,	Crave Feedback,
	Question Authority	Team Oriented

The Reasons for Generational Differences

There are the inevitable changes that occur as cultures and societies develop, such as increased efficiency and evolution of thought. The evolution is usually toward a kinder, more gentle and inclusive way of seeing the world and its inhabitants. If one was to characterize the differences between the Traditional Generation, the Baby Boomers, Generation X and Generation Y it would be summarized as a kinder and more gentle, inclusive way of viewing the world of management, and especially family. But how has this happened?

Socialization, living arrangements, economy, work, technology, consumerism, and family and cultural diversity are the aspects of this change we will investigate to first understand the differences.

Second, we will try to understand how we can adapt and assimilate all generations into a cohesive work unit. The key is to understand what made these generational groups different and how those differences affect the way they see the world, and work.

Socialization in short is to fit into or train for a social environment, to adapt to social needs, or to participate actively in a social group. With each group of people the diversity in which they grew up was very different, and because of these differences, these groups have adapted in different ways to their environment.

> *"A society that lives on the river, will be good swimmers and fishermen, while another society that lives in the plains will be good hunters and farmers. The environments in which socialization occurred are different so they adapt differently."*

The statistics below will shed light on why one group seeks independence and the other group is dependent, and why one group may value family and the other may value work.

Generational Differences

Socialization

Baby Boomers
- First TV sets
- Were cared for by their mothers mostly—and at home.

Generation X
- Spent 12,000 lifetime hours in front of a teacher and 20,000 lifetime hours in front of a TV.
- Were socialized by the TV and in some cases it taught them to tie their shoes, count, and spell while both parents worked.
- The first generation to have no legal segregation in their lifetime.

Generation Y
- Nurtured and pampered by parents, socialized by computers, and technology is part of life.
- Is of the "No Person Left Behind" Generation.

Living Arrangements

Baby Boomers
- Own homes, and live alone mostly, (except for their Generation X'er children who can't leave the house.)

Generation X
- X'ers can't leave home and it's not because they don't have ideas of personal freedom and independence it's because of economics.
- Often when X'ers do move out, they move in with friends of either gender and with many of them.
- Gen X'ers have waited longer than any other generation to get married.

Generation Y
- Generation Y is just now entering the workforce with many of the same constraints as Gen X'ers. They mostly live at home or with groups of friends. They are just starting careers.
- With the oldest members of Generation Y (those in their mid to late 20s) starting to enter the housing market, the characteristics of this demanding, strong-willed generation provide many clues to their preferences in living arrangements. For instance, they:
  -Favor the quirky, unique and different.
  -Seek diversity in all aspects of their lives.
  -Prefer urban over suburban environments.
  -Multi-task (One observation: 'Most don't wear watches because watches only do one thing.'" Trisha Riggs, The Ground Floor, http://thegroundfloor.typepad.com

Economics

Baby Boomers
- BBer's are postponing retirement because of economics which is halting the career progressions of Gen X'ers and making entrance into the workforce more difficult for Generation Y.

Generation X
- X'ers__have faced economic uncertainty their entire lives—recession in the 80's and 2000's, junk bonds and ever increasing deficit. X'ers are not doing as well in real terms as the BBer's that came before them.

Generation Y
- Entering a volatile job market, with global competition, world crisis, high unemployment and a workforce that won't or can't retire.

Work

Baby Boomers
- BBer's hold power and authority in companies and are motivated by position, perks and prestige. They sacrificed a great deal for work and in some cases their families. Workaholics—they believe younger generations should conform to a culture of overwork. Do not question authority. Believe in face time at the office, and have difficulty adjusting to flexibility trends.

Generation X
- They have been laid-off, unemployed, downsized, right-sized and outsourced. They want a balance between work and life and for the first time a generation is, "Working to live, rather than living to work."
- The Social Contract has failed them time and time again.

Generation Y
- Generation Y are not afraid to question authority and will sacrifice money and prestige for a better work/life balance.
- Prioritize family over work.
- Value flexibility.

Technology

Baby Boomers
- The average age for baby-boomers to start using computers—some still don't know how to use a computer.

Generation X
- Work and technology are intertwined. The average age at which they started using computers was 9.

Generation Y
- Generation Y grew up with technology and relies on it to perform jobs better and for personal entertainment. They would rather text or email than have a face-to face conversation.
- It is who they are.

Family

Baby Boomers
- Many female Boomers entered the workforce leaving latch key kids—Gen X'ers to fend for themselves after school and on weekends.

Generation X
- Top three signs of a good life—Home, Happy Marriage, and Children.
- In many cases by age 16 they were living in non-traditional families headed by a single parent, or families composed of children from multiple marriages which is probably why family is so important to them.

Generation Y
- Prioritizes family over work and will work less and make less for a better work/life balance.

As we unravel the changes occurring between the generations, and start to understand what makes them tick, what they value and what makes them happy we start to see new research into work-life balance. Each generation's ideas toward work change and personal happiness is coming to the forefront of what people need from work.

"We believe we should work to be happy,
but could that be backwards?" (Shawn Achor)

Shawn Achor is a Harvard Professor where he is the winner of over a dozen distinguished teaching awards and where he delivered lectures on positive psychology in the most popular class at Harvard.

Shawn Achor—"*The Happy Secret to Better Work*"
http://www.ted.com/talks/lang/en/shawn_achor_the_happy_secret_to_better_work.html

The changes that occur in the workforce with each new generation that comes of age continue to perplex the exiting generation. The new ideas of management are described below. Work doesn't have to be drudgery, as Shawn Achor explained above.

"We all have the capacity for great things if we can develop the
right environments for work to close the gaps between what
people want and what they are getting from work."

The Changing Management Paradigm

The Changing Management Paradigm is a new way of looking at the management of people. It is not something that was created because someone thought it was a good idea; it is in response to the generational changes occurring and the evolution of our society and the way each generation views work. The changes are occurring due to the shift in generational leadership and what people need from work. The largest gap between people isn't race, religion, income or education, it is generational.

The old way of doing business is called an **Authoritarian Style of Management** which separates power at different levels in the organization. Authoritarian management believes that power should exist in an organization at the upper levels but not at the lower levels. Employees should not question commands from above. Baby-Boomers are accustomed to this style of management. Often they make the mistake of demanding the same from younger generations that don't subscribe to this thought process and especially that style of management.

Inherent to Authoritarianism is the **Assumption of Irresponsibility**, or the assumption that management makes regarding employees; that they are not competent to make decisions about their work-life when in reality they are productive, responsible tax-paying parents, spouses and friends.

Theory X is a philosophy of management that is embraced by authoritarian organizations. It has been proven counter-effective in most modern practice. Management assumes employees are lazy and will avoid work if they can and inherently dislike work. As a result, management believes that workers need to be closely supervised and comprehensive systems of control need to be in place. It espouses that employees will avoid responsibility when possible. Many people interpret Theory X as a negative set of beliefs about employees.

The new way of doing business is called a **Learning Organization** which embraces flattened hierarchies, teams, employee empowerment, strategy formulation, and cultural equality. Learning organizations embrace the **Theory Y** philosophy of management in which management assumes employees will be ambitious, self-motivated and exercise self-control. It is believed that employees enjoy mental and physical work duties. At the heart of this theory is the belief that work is as natural as play and that each are necessary to be a healthy human being. Employees possess the ability for creative problem solving, but their talents are often underused in organizations. Given the proper conditions, Theory Y managers believe that employees will learn to seek out and accept responsibility, exercise self-control and self-direction in accomplishing objectives to which they are committed. A Theory Y manager believes that, given the right conditions, most people want to do well at work. They believe that the satisfaction of doing a good job is strong motivator. Many people interpret Theory Y as a positive set of beliefs about employees.

Now, let's look at the characteristics of the new paradigm of management, the learning organization. Many of these ideas will be difficult for some Baby-Boomer managers to embrace because many were "brought up" under the old, authoritarian approach to management. Many of the issues managers and employees encounter today are because of authoritarian managers who prescribe to Theory X, clash with employees who need a manager that subscribes to Theory Y and the principles of a learning organization. Remember, it is the leader who must adapt to the changing times, not just the employee.

Characteristics of a Learning Organization

1. **Company Leadership** has to buy-in to the ideas and practices that make up a learning organization. The first thing is to develop a **flattened hierarchy** which means power and control does not rest solely at the top of the hierarchy. In fact, the hierarchy is squished so that if decisions do need to go the top, there are fewer levels to negotiate.

> *"Leaders don't have to have every answer or solution they just need to be the one who knows the right answer or solution when they hear it."*

2. **Teams** should be formed to solve problems at a functional level, administrative level and strategic level. If people feel as if they have a say and some control of their work-life and can execute the solutions to problems with their team, they feel a sense of ownership, buy-in and community. They won't want to let their team members down and they tend to self-monitor each other.

> *"Small bands of people are created to make big things happen because the weaknesses of the individual are absorbed by the group."*

3. **Employee Empowerment**—Employees must be able to make functional decisions without having to check with someone else. For an employee to feel fully empowered the following characteristics must be present:

    A. **Access to information**—employees want to understand how their piece of the puzzle fits into the overall organizational puzzle. To understand how their piece fits into the organization helps employees find meaning in their work.

"To view an entire painting is much more rewarding than viewing just the top left corner."

B. **Accountability**—employees, if given the right tools, guidelines and freedom to find success, will find success and they will even monitor and control their own success.

"Being accountable to one's self is the strongest, most lasting motivation toward success."

C. **Participation**—employees do not want to feel that decisions are made for them, but by them, and with their input.

"When you have a problem, ask your employees for the solution . . . time after time I have seen businesses struggle when the solution to problems were known by employees." (Jack Shewmaker, former President of Wal-Mart)

D. **Innovation**—employees need to be encouraged to try new ideas, processes and ways of doing business. This means that there has to be tolerance for trial and error. So often we expect perfection the first time. Remember, Thomas Edison developed over 1000 light bulbs that didn't work properly. Thank goodness he had the spirit of innovation and didn't get discouraged by failure.

"It is with each failure our focus on success becomes more acute."

"What made you successful in the past, won't in the future." (Lew Platt, Hewlett Packard CEO and founder)

4. Strategy Formulation—employees should be asked for input to develop strategies for success. This also helps gain buy-in from employees when it becomes time to implement the strategy.

> *"If they would just ask me, I could tell them what needs done."*

5. Cultural Equality—employees at all levels should be treated equally and fairly. There should not be a hierarchy that exists where one person is more important to the team than another. In healthcare, this discrepancy often occurs between caregivers. For example, the duties that a Registered Nurse (RN) performs as compared to a Licensed Practical Nurse (LPN) as compared to a Patient Care Assistant (PCA) are very different, and have different value. The key is that each position depends on the other and neither can do their job without the other. For this reason, each member of the team has equal importance and they should be consulted, and given a say in each decision as it relates to their work environment. A change in an RN's role will certainly have an impact on a PCA's role. To make a change in the RN's role without consulting the PCA to see how the change will affect them is a recipe for disaster.

Each person on the team has a job to do for the success of the team. Those jobs are valued differently, and paid accordingly, but that isn't what is important, what is, is that no one can do their job without the other, so under this model, importance is equal, value or pay is different, but at no time, can one do their job without the assistance of another. If one fails, they all fail.

> *"A car must have an engine, drive shaft, wheels,*
> *steering wheel and driver to be effective.*
> *An engine is useless without a drive shaft to*
> *turn the wheels. Wheels are useless without*
> *a steering wheel to guide them. The steering*
> *wheel is useless without a driver to direct the car."*

The Leaders Role in Employee Development—Maslow's Needs Hierarchy of Motivation

A leader's primary role is to grow people through developing their skills, abilities and knowledge. It is through teaching and training that employees prepare for greater responsibility. It is the leader's job to keep employees intellectually stimulated and always reaching for a higher goal.

> *"Stagnation breeds discontent and decay, and challenge breeds responsibility and growth."*

The pyramid that follows illustrates the most primal needs at the bottom and then the more advanced needs toward the tip of the pyramid. The key to understanding the needs hierarchy as described by Maslow is that a lower level need must be obtained prior to a higher level need.

> *"One cannot be concerned with self-esteem if they are sitting in the rain, starving and thirsty."*

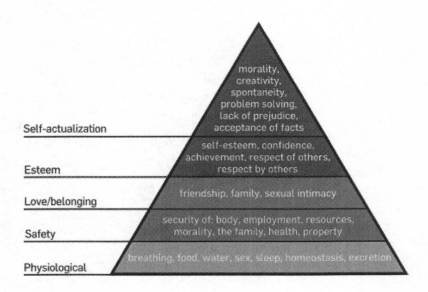

Self-actualization — morality, creativity, spontaneity, problem solving, lack of prejudice, acceptance of facts

Esteem — self-esteem, confidence, achievement, respect of others, respect by others

Love/belonging — friendship, family, sexual intimacy

Safety — security of: body, employment, resources, morality, the family, health, property

Physiological — breathing, food, water, sex, sleep, homeostasis, excretion

> *"A leader's primary focus should be to inspire greatness."*

14

Needs Hierarchy as related to Work—The Leader's Mission

Physiological Needs—Obtaining employment will provide shelter, food and water. Sex will need to be found outside of work. But honestly, the likelihood is greater if the person has a job.

Safety Needs—Employment will provide a means to maintaining food and shelter on an on-going basis and the result is that safety is satisfied.

Social Needs—Employment is a venue for establishing social networks and friends.

Self-Esteem Needs—Mutually valuable and respectful relationships between the employee and leadership will foster achievement, recognition and respect from others. This is the level at which a leader can have a positive effect on an employee's perception of themselves and the organization. If employees feel good about themselves, they feel better about work.

Self-Actualization Needs—It should be the goal of all leaders to make their employees the best they can be and then encourage them to move into another more challenging role. This is the most dynamic aspect of the needs hierarchy and it can change over time as a person grows and develops. The goal is to keep employees at the self-esteem level, and always striving to be the best they can be through self-actualization. This will make for productive, engaged and long-term employees. There isn't a blueprint to self-actualization, each person is different. Good leadership, through discussions with employees will help each employee set a course to self-actualization, reach it and move onto the next challenge.

Diversity is what causes change; different ideas spark other ideas which can often lead to innovative improvement. The question we need to be concerned with as leaders is how we react to it. Do we embrace it and tap into it for a different perspective, even if it means we may have to change our style of management? The answer to this question is the critical piece to this puzzle. We can keep banging our head against the wall or we can adapt and find another way over the wall.

Chapter 2—Effective Communication

A Brief Communication Overview

"Talking to you is like clapping with one hand."

The above quote is too often how conversations go in our world. With one hand, no sound is emitted, therefore clapping has not occurred. Communication is no different, it takes two parties to communicate—one must send a message and at least one person must receive the message. Simply hearing the message is considerably different than listening and understanding the message. In all cases, each person that hears a message perceives different meaning.

"Meaning is in the mind." (Lesikar, Flately, 13)

This creates an inconsistency in the message sent and the message received and then an even deeper inconsistency is created if there are multiple people receiving the same message.

"Our goal is to minimize inconsistency
in the communication process."

Communication is a dynamic process that has many levels and layers of understanding. For a message to be received and understood there has to be a sender and a receiver. For successful communication, the receiver has to take from the message the sender's intent.

For example, if you picked up the phone and on the other end a voice spoke Russian to you, and you didn't speak Russian, communication would not have occurred. To help understand, the communication process is outlined below.

The Process of Human Communication

1. **A Message is Sent**—this begins the process of communication. Someone conceptualizes a message and speaks it.

2. **Sensory World**—a message must enter the receiver's sensory world—hearing, smell, taste, touch, sight.

3. **Detection**—the message is detected through stimulation of the senses and the main consideration at this point in the communication process is how acutely tuned in to the message the receiver is. Is it actually stimulating or is it "white noise?"

"In one ear and right out the other."

4. **Filtering**—the message has entered the sensory world and has been detected, now it is filtered by everything the receiver has done, heard, seen, touched, and experienced in their lifetime. Meaning is assigned to the message as it relates to the receivers reference points. This is the point in which miscommunication occurs.

"Everyone has different life experiences; therefore everyone takes different meaning from every message. The goal is to be clear and concise in your message."

5. **Response Formation**—if the message was received and meaning was given to the message in a sufficiently strong way, a response will be developed. This is the most complex aspect of communication.

"There is evidence that the ability to respond meaningfully, is related to one's intelligence and the extent that one permits the mind to react. The ability to evaluate filtered information and formulate meaning also is related to language ability."
(Lesikar, Flately, 11)

Non-Verbal and Verbal Communication

There are two main avenues by which people communicate face-to-face—Non-Verbal and Verbal Communications. Research indicates that 85% of communication is conveyed through non-verbal cues during a face-to-face conversation, such as tone of voice, posture, body language and facial expressions. This means that verbal communication represents only 15% of the message we convey during an oral communication. **Verbal Communication**, the words used in communication have meaning in definitional form. It is difficult to misinterpret the word, "Dog." Generally, without seeing the person say the word, you conjure an image of a dog—probably your dog if you have one. Still, you would have no idea how the person felt about dogs. But what if you saw and heard someone say, "Dog," in a high pitched voice while leaning down to the dog? You may get the point that they are very fond of the dog.

Non-Verbal Communication is the way we present words through **body language, space, time and paralanguage**. It is where 85% of the message is communicated. These are non-verbal cues and these cues can indicate a positive or negative intent to the message and can indicate truth, lies, apprehension and in fact, every other human emotion. People are very keen when it comes to understanding non-verbal cues. They may not be able to verbalize the understanding, but it is there, deep in their minds. Through the millennia we've become master sensors of human interaction.

> *"Non-verbal communication is the most ancient form of human communication. We intuit and perceive the true meaning of a message through body language. We just need to trust it."*

Amy Cuddy is a Social Psychologist and Associate Professor in the Negotiations, Organizations and Markets Unit at the Harvard Business School. She has proven through her research that our body language can be used to change who we are. If we take a certain posture, hormone levels actually change and convince our minds that we are confident and powerful. Thereby, enhancing how we behave and ultimately changing the outcomes for the better just through changing how we present ourselves.

Amy Cuddy—"*Your Body Language Shapes Who You Are*"
http://www.ted.com/talks/lang/en/amy_cuddy_your_body_language_shapes_who_you_are.html

> "*Our non-verbals govern how we think and feel about ourselves.*"
> (Amy Cuddy)

> "*Our bodies change our minds*
> . . . *and our minds change our behavior*
> . . . *and our behavior changes our outcomes.*" (Amy Cuddy)

If body language is so powerful, as Amy Cuddy illustrated through her research, wouldn't it be wonderful if we were able to use this not only to our advantage, but to the advantage of everyone around us?

> "*Do not underestimate the power of non-verbal communication. Use it to help you communicate better, affect change positively, and increase the satisfaction you and others obtain from work.*"

Body Language—When we wave our arms or fingers, wrinkle our foreheads, stand erect, smile, gaze at another, and so on, we convey certain meanings. In particular, the face and eyes, gestures, posture, and physical appearance reflect the inner workings of emotions in our bodies. (*Lesikar, Flatley,* 409)

> "*A picture is worth a thousand words.*"

Space—the space between two people can indicate how comfortable they are with each other, how much they trust one another and in fact space language communicates just like body language. Many experts agree that there are four different types of space:

"It is uncomfortable if the space people share is not agreed upon."

1. **Intimate**—Physical Contact—18 inches
2. **Personal**—18 inches—4 feet
3. **Social**—4 feet—12 feet
4. **Public**—12 feet to the range of seeing or hearing

Time Language—communicates to people in how you respond to appointments, requests, meetings, and whether or not you respect another's time. When time is shared by people and one party's time is not respected, a clear, negative non-verbal cue is being sent.

"You can wait. Don't you know I am more important than you?"

Paralanguage—is the way words are said and emphasized. Paralanguage is closest to communication with words because it is how certain words are said or emphasized. Read the examples below and emphasize the underlined words to illustrate the differences in meaning of each sentence even though the same words are used.

<u>You</u> communicate well with me.   You <u>communicate</u> well with me.

You communicate <u>well</u> with me.   You communicate well with <u>me.</u>

"You're putting the wrong **em 'pha sis** *on the* wrong **syl 'la ble.** *"*
(Mike Meyers)

Take a look at the additional scenarios below as an example as to how the same words can have two totally different meanings given the body language that is exhibited.

Negative Non-Verbal Cues

Jane stood with her hands on her hips and glared at Jack. Her eyebrows were furrowed and all her weight rested on her left leg. Her right foot pointed out and away.

Jack said, "It's how you look at me, that makes me feel this way."

Her head tilted sideways. Her eyes opened wide and she looked upward. Her palms flipped to the sky and her arms stretched outward. She said, "Yeah, I'm sure you're right, Jack."

"It wasn't what she said that made me mad;
it was how she said it."

Positive Non-Verbal Cues

Jane stood with her hands loosely clasped in front of her. She faced Jack and both feet pointed directly at him. Her posture was straight and she gazed into Jack's eyes.

Jack said, "It's the way you look at me that makes me feel this way."

A smile crossed her face and she focused deeper into Jack's eyes. She nodded her head unconsciously and slow. She said, "Yeah, I'm sure you're right, Jack."

"It wasn't what she said that made me fall in love;
it was how she said it."

Verbal Communication

The key to increasing communication effectiveness is to ensure verbal cues and non-verbal cues are aligned. If there is inconsistency, it may leave the listener befuddled. Sarcasm is an example that is often sent through inconsistent verbal and non-verbal messages. The words do not align with the tone of the voice and poor word choice can lead the listener to a negative conclusion. The same message can either be conveyed positively or negatively. It is a matter of word choice.

Negative Word Choice	**Positive Word Choice**
You **failed** to complete the consent for your **surgery**. We **can't** do the **surgery without** signed consent.	To **insure** you **understand** your **procedure, please** look over your consent form. If you have any questions, please let me answer them for you. Be sure to sign the bottom. **Thanks!**
There is **no** smoking on this campus. You **must** go to the street around the corner.	This is a smoke-free campus. You **may** smoke in the designated area around the corner.
We **cannot** do the **surgery until** Friday.	We would be **happy to do** the **procedure** on Friday.

"Taking a moment to communicate with positive words may take a bit longer, but the reward is that you may be able to keep a patient or customer from becoming irritated, threatened or scared. But most importantly, if you invest time and energy on the front-end, the back-end runs smoother."

Positive and Negative Communication Styles

People either learn to communicate or choose to communicate with certain styles. There is evidence that behaviors may not reflect a person's "traits or personality," so much as they reflect the situations in which people find themselves. *(Myers, Myers, 97-98.)*

This is similar to the idea of **contingent leadership** which we will discuss in the next chapter. The situation determines how we behave and our behavior in a certain situation determines the outcome and the outcome determines the success of the situation.

People tend to use different styles to accomplish their own initiatives or agendas. Often we employ a negative communication style when our arguments are not strong. This alienates people and leaves them feeling as if they have been taken advantage of, insulted or demeaned. Remember, particularly, the up and coming generations prefer a participative style of management in which their voices are heard, they are given an opportunity to ask questions and seek clarification.

"The younger generation wants to know
the "why" behind their actions."

If an employee is given a say in the process and their ideas or input are not only heard but considered and possibly incorporated, the likelihood of gaining buy-in from them has increased tremendously.

If in business, the goals of the manager are aligned with the goals of the employee there is no good reason not to sincerely ask an employee's opinion on what should be done and how it should be done. Remember, the leader doesn't have to have all the answers; they just need to recognize a better solution when it is presented. The most effective way to do this is to use the assertive style of communication as illustrated below. The negative communication styles that leave employees feeling used and abused are illustrated so that you may understand them and avoid them.

The following communication styles illustrate positive and negative approaches to communication in the decision making process.

In this table, the question content could be almost anything. You could be working out how to ask for a raise, how to talk to another person about a poor process, how to decide who takes which assignments or any other small or large decision. Assume for this example, that the question is; "What movie should we go see?"

Style	Statement	Translation
Aggressive	"Only one movie in town is any good We'll go to that one."	"My way or nothing.
Placating-	"Whatever movie you want to see is fine with me."	"Poor dumb me; I'm really helpless."
Intellectual-	"Reviews say that the new French film is directed, acted and filmed well, and is a "must."	"I have no feelings about it myself, only the intellectual advice from others."
Manipulative-	"I'm not sure I want to go to a movie."	Coax me; I want to be in a position of deciding by playing hard-to-get.
Assertive-	"I'm most interested in the new Robert Redford movie. How about you?	"Here's what I want. What do you want?"

(Myers, Myers 98)

"An assertive communicator is confident and open to other's ideas. It isn't about being right; it is about sharing one's perspective and then listening to another's perspective. Generally, somewhere in the middle lies the best solution for both parties."

Listening

"Talking to you is like clapping with one hand."

Most of us have felt ignored by our co-workers, friends, spouses and others. Then, other times we feel like these same people, "just get us." Think about the times when you felt ignored and then think about the times you felt syncopation. What were the differences? Most likely it was that the person you were talking to actively listened to you. Not having someone listen to you, especially a manager or supervisor, leaves the employee feeling unappreciated, undervalued, and ignored. These feelings lead to increased turnover in work life . . . and divorce in personal life.

The most underrated communication skill is **listening**. Most people want to talk and while they are in the middle of a conversation are, instead of listening, gearing up for what they are going to say in rebuttal. There are public speaking courses in universities, but there are few improved listening courses. Some research suggests that we only listen with 25% effectiveness. *(Guffey, 4)*. What is the point of improving speaking skills if no one is going to listen anyway? The improvement isn't needed in the message. It's needed in the listener. With 25% effectiveness this creates a tremendous opportunity for large improvements in communication.

There are two main ways people listen. One is easy and the other is hard and much effort has to be exerted for listening effectiveness. This is likely why people are generally poor listeners. **Passive Listening** and **Active Listening** are two wildly different ideas.

Passive Listening is what you would do if you wanted to make your employees feel undervalued, underappreciated and frustrated. It is what you do when there is a radio in the background of your home, or car. You hear it, but you are not exactly absorbing the lyrics and certainly not the meaning of the lyrics. If you are a parent, you know what passive listening looks like. It is the look your child gives you when they are in trouble. They nod their head at you and kind of look around sadly and jiggle something in their hands.

Many of you have probably seen this phenomenon and asked the child, "What did I just say?" The child is then snapped back into reality and the glaze over their eyes clears and they look like a bright-eyed child again, at least for another ten seconds. If they were listening with purpose, they would be able to rattle off what your message to them was, "DON'T THROW ROCKS AT YOUR BROTHER!"

So instead, you have to say it again and refocus their attention on what you are saying. The difference between a nine year old and a thirty-nine year old is thirty years, but why isn't there thirty years of improvement?

"It's hard work to be a good listener. <u>You must decide to do it.</u>"

As a manager, you should avoid passive listening at all costs. The price you will pay is tremendous as it relates to loss of trust, respect, and buy-in. Employees are aware when they are not being listened to—they see the haze over your eyes, like the glaze on a donut. The goal is to be an **active listener.**

> *"Active listeners participate in the communication process. They take an interest in the communicator, the message and the meaning of the message."*

Active Listening

The list that follows was developed by an anonymous author, and has often been cited and quoted over the years.

The Ten Commandments of Active Listening

1. **Stop Talking**—Unfortunately, most of us prefer talking to listening. Even when we are not talking, we are inclined to concentrate on what to say next rather than on listening to others. You must stop talking before you can listen.
2. **Put the Speaker at Ease**—If you make the speaker feel at ease, he or she will do a better job of talking. Then you will have better input to work with.
3. **Show the Speaker You Want to Listen**—If the speaker sees you are listening to understand, rather than oppose, you will create a climate for information exchange. You should look interested and be interested. Doing things like reading, looking at your watch, checking your smart phone and looking away distracts the speaker.
4. **Remove Distractions**—The things you do also can distract the speaker. So don't doodle, tap with your pencil, shuffle papers or the like.
5. **Empathize with the Speaker**—If you place yourself in the speaker's position and look at things from the speaker's point of view, you will help create a climate of understanding that can result in a true exchange of information.

6. **Be Patient**—You will need to allow the speaker plenty of time. Remember, not everyone can get to the point as quickly and clearly as you. Do not interrupt. Interruptions are barriers to the exchange of information.

7. **Hold Your Temper**—From our knowledge of the workings of our minds we know that anger impedes communication. Angry people build walls between each other. They harden their position and block their minds to the words of others.

8. **Go Easy on Argument and Criticism**—Argument and criticism tend to put the speaker on the defensive. He or she then tends to "clam up" or get angry. Thus, even if you win the argument, you lose. Rarely does either party benefit from argument and criticism.

9. **Ask Questions**—By frequently asking questions, you display an open mind and show that you are listening and thereby assist the speaker in developing his or her message and in improving the correctness of meaning.

10. **STOP TALKING**—The last commandment is to stop talking. It was also the first. All the other commandments depend on it. (Lesikar, Flately, 407)

"You must know the other person's viewpoint
before you can respond intelligently."

Additional Tips for Active Listening

Provide Verbal Feedback

1. Ask relevant questions at appropriate times.
2. Allow the person to know you are listening, by giving a simple, "uh-huh, OK, or right."
3. Saying, "I understand" goes a long way in getting people to be open. It doesn't mean you agree. It just means you hear and understand what they are saying.

Non-Verbal Affirmation of Listening—This is what you can do to let people know you are hearing them and actively listening without saying a word.

1. Nod your head in the affirmative
2. Maintain eye contact, but do not stare
3. Present yourself with open posture
   A. Face the person
   B. Smile
   C. Do not cross your arms
   D. Do not turn away from the person
   E. Do not tap your foot or hand—this indicates impatience.

Patterns of Communication—Giving Good and Bad News—Verbal and Written

In your role as manager, you may be called upon to write memos, letters or other forms of communication in addition to just speaking. There are two different approaches to developing your message both orally and written. The approach depends on how the information you are sharing is going to be received.

To put it in a nutshell, it depends on whether the message is positive or negative. The **direct pattern** of communication is used for good or neutral messages and the **indirect pattern** is used for negative or persuasive messages.

The direct and indirect patterns of communication can be used in written and verbal messages. Below you will see examples of both direct and indirect communication styles.

Direct Pattern of Communication—(for Good News and Neutral News)

A. **Begin with the Objective**—If you are seeking information, start asking for it. If you are sharing good news, say it.

B. **Present a Necessary Explanation**—Explain why you are requesting the information or why the news is good.

C. **End with a Goodwill Statement**—End the communication with a statement of goodwill because this is normally how friendly people handle these situations. (*Lesiker, Flately,* 100-101)

<u>**Example**</u>**—The Direct Pattern**—you must tell someone they are going to be promoted.

Begin with the Objective

"Congratulations, you got the promotion you applied for."

Necessary Explanation

"There were a lot of applicants, but your experience, innovation, creativity and longevity set you apart."

Goodwill Statement

"This is a terrific honor and I know you'll be great. Thanks for applying."

Indirect Pattern of Communication—(For Bad News, Proposals, Persuasive Messages, or Refusals)

A. **Begin with a Strategic Buffer**—Use words that set up the strategy to overcome or reduce the impact of the negative message that follows.

B. **Develop a Strategy**—Make this as logical and convincing as you can. Use words and reasoning that emphasize the reader's viewpoint. You are going to want to **"Answer the Why"** in this section of the communication strategy.

C. **Present the Bad News Positively**—After you have buffered the bad news, try to understand the reader's viewpoint, minimize a negative response and give the bad news as positively as possible.

D. **End with a Positive Note**—Even a skillfully crafted bad news presentation is likely to put the reader in an unhappy frame of mind; you should end the message with a happy or positive note. Your goal is to shift the person's thoughts to happier things. (Lesiker, Flately, 101-102)

<u>**Example**</u>**—The Indirect Pattern**—you must tell someone they are not going to be promoted.

Strategic Buffer

"A lot of qualified people applied for this position.

Strategy Development

"Many of them had excellent skills and some differentiated themselves because of their longevity, creativity, innovation and specific experience to the needs of the position."

Presenting the Bad News Positively
"There will be a time when you are the most qualified person for this position, but at this time however, someone else was more qualified."

Ending with a Positive Note
"Keep working hard and gaining experience and if you ever have questions or need clarification on anything, please let me know."

The key to good communication is to understand what it looks and sounds like, and then practice it. It isn't easy for most people or the statistics would be different.

"Good communication is the single most cited reason for business success."

It isn't technical knowledge or education; it is whether or not managers and employees can communicate accurately, openly, concisely and with mutual respect. The simple act of actively listening illustrates concern, interest and the desire to understand the employee's perspective. It makes people feel valued, and valued employees are good productive, engaged employees.

Chapter 3—The Differences Between Leadership and Management

Overview on Leadership and Management

Management and Leadership are often erroneously used synonymously. They are, in fact, nothing alike. Management requires the influencing of tangible things, and leadership requires the influencing of emotion, spirit, motivation and other intangible aspects. It is what makes the topic so enigmatic and so difficult to explain from a theoretical perspective. We are left with a bunch of quotes on leadership, and examples of good leadership, but we are not exactly sure how to prescribe leadership. The difference between management and leadership is the difference between the role of a prison warden and the role of a major league baseball manager.

> *"**Management** is telling people what to do according to prescribed parameters. **Leadership** is getting people to support what needs to happen and making them feel good about making it happen."*

John Kotter of the Harvard Business School argues that **Management** is about coping with complexity. Good management brings order and consistency by drawing up formal plans, designing rigid structures and monitoring results against the plans. **Leadership** in contrast, is about coping with change. Leaders establish direction and develop a vision of the future; then they align people by communicating this vision and inspiring them to overcome hurdles.

Like our example of the Warden and MLB Manager, the warden sets rules, and ensures they are obeyed. He is the metaphor for Management. He certainly isn't inspiring criminals to greatness, and maybe that's one fundamental flaw with our prison system but, on the other hand, the MLB Manager is the metaphor for Leadership. He is not really teaching his players anything, or setting rules, he is simply trying to find ways to get the most from his team and inspire a shared vision, mission and goals which ideally culminates in a World Series appearance. The MLB Manager wants his players to be creative and innovative and approach the game of baseball as a team using each of their strengths for the good of the mission, the World Series.

> ***Management*** *is ensuring a group of people adhere to policies and procedures.*
> ***Leadership*** *is the intangible actions of people that inspire greatness."*

These intangibles of leadership inspire people to not only follow policies and procedures but also to think in terms of what can be done to accomplish our goals in creative and innovative ways. It inspires people to do what some never thought possible; find little nuggets of greatness in themselves and share those with the world, which in turn inspires greatness in others. Those people then dig into themselves for their own nuggets of greatness to share with the world. The idea is that greatness inspires greatness—that's leadership.

In organizing and staffing, **Management** focuses on providing a structure to the work of individuals, their relationships in the organization, and the physical context in which they work. It includes placing people in the right jobs and developing rules and procedures for how the work is to be performed. For **Leadership**, organizing and staffing take the form of communicating a vision to employees, invoking their commitment, and working with them to build teams and coalitions useful in fulfilling the organization's mission, (Northouse, 8-9)

> *"Leadership is like water. It is abstract in that it takes many forms and reacts to its surroundings. Management is like stone. It is tangible, in that it takes one form and its surroundings react to it. Like water, leadership changes as soon as you grasp it and drips away. Like stone, management is easily grasped and stays firm. Water inspires creativity and innovation*

to spawn. Stone refuses to let ideas take root like gravel at
the water's edge. Leadership is the mist that envelopes us.
Management is the cell that contains us. In fire, water turns
to steam, calms the fire and comes back again just as strong.
In fire, stone doesn't budge, but cracks and crumbles from heat
and deteriorates. The collective power of water breaks down
stone, yet stone can never break down water."

The reason it is so difficult to theorize leadership or give a step-by-step explanation as to how to become a leader is because, as one may imagine, leadership is something that happens all the time and varies with each decision on a moment to moment basis. It is fluid like water. It is organic and complex and requires constant reevaluation. To explain how someone illustrated good leadership would mean being able to decode the workings of their brain. Instead, what we are left with are characteristics of leaders, examples of leaders and a few models as to what characteristics and traits leaders have and how they fall within a given style of leadership.

"Management is easy. Leadership is hard.
It is easy to make rules and enforce them.
It is difficult to get people to want to follow them."

Leadership Styles

Charismatic Leadership—(John F. Kennedy, Martin Luther King Jr., Steve Jobs, Mary Kay Ash, Ted Turner, Bill Clinton)

Charismatic Leadership Theory states that followers make attributions of heroic or extraordinary leadership abilities when they observe certain behaviors. Five characteristics of the charismatic leader have been isolated:

1. **Vision and Articulation**: Has a vision—expressed as an idealized goal—that proposes a future better than the status quo and is able to clarify the importance of the vision in terms that are understandable to others.

2. **Personal Risk**: Willing to take on high personal risk, incur high costs and engage in self-sacrifice to achieve the vision.
3. **Environmental Sensitivity**: Able to make realistic assessments of the environmental constraints and resources needed to bring about change.
4. **Sensitivity to Follower Needs**: Perceptive of others' abilities and responsive to their needs and feelings.
5. **Unconventional Behavior:** Engages in behaviors that are perceived as novel and counter to norms. (Robbins, 343)

Transactional Leadership—These are leaders who guide or motivate their followers in the direction of established goals by clarifying role and task requirements.

Transformational Leadership—are leaders who inspire followers to transcend their own self-interests and who are capable of having a profound and extraordinary effect on followers.
Transformational leadership is built on top of Transactional Leadership and the two should not be viewed as opposing ways of getting things done but, generally, you do not get to transformation, without transaction.

In other words, if you view these latter two types of leadership and separate out their essence, you will notice that Transactional Leadership is more like Management and Transformational Leadership is more in line with our former definitions of Leadership. Again, we often use the two words synonymously when, the fact remains, you can call it whatever you want, but there are differences between managers and leaders.

> *"Managers aren't always leaders,*
> *and leaders aren't always managers.*
> *It is the ability to get things done and make people feel good*
> *about it that makes a leader a leader—not a title."*

Evidence supports the superiority of transformational leadership over transactional leadership with impressive consistency. For example, a number of studies with US, Canadian, and German military officers found, at every level, that transformational leaders were evaluated as more effective than their transactional counterparts. And Managers at FedEX who were rated by their followers as exhibiting more transformational leadership were evaluated by their immediate supervisors as higher performers and more promotable. In summary, the overall evidence indicates that transformational leadership is more strongly correlated than transactional leadership with lower turnover rates, higher productivity and higher employee satisfaction. (Robbins, 344)

Characteristics of Transactional and Transformational Leaders

Transactional Leader—(Management)

- Contingent Reward—Contracts the exchange of rewards for effort, promises rewards for good performance, and recognizes accomplishments.
- Management by Exception—(Active)—Watches and searches for deviations from rules and standards and takes corrective action.
- Management by Exception—(Passive)—Intervenes only if standards are not met.
- Laissez Faire—Abdicates responsibilities, avoids making decisions.

Transformational Leader—(Leadership)

- Charisma—Provides vision and sense of mission, instills pride, gains respect and trust.
- Inspiration—Communicates high expectations, uses symbols to focus efforts, expresses important purposes in simple ways.
- Intellectual Stimulation—Promotes intelligence, rationality, and careful problem solving.
- Individualized Consideration—Gives personal attention, treats each employee individually, coaches and advises. (Robbins, 344)

Visionary Leadership—(Examples,—Michael Dell, Rupert Murdoch, Mary Kay Ash)

Visionary Leadership is the ability to create and articulate a realistic, credible, attractive vision of the future for an organization or organizational unit that grows out of and improves upon the present. This vision, if properly selected and implemented, is so energizing that it in effect jump-starts the future by calling forth the skills, talents and resources to make it happen.

Generally, there have been three leadership traits that visionary leader's exhibit.

1. **Excellent Communicator**—the ability to explain the vision to others.
2. **Integrity**—Express the vision not only through words, but behavior.
3. **Extend the vision to different contexts**—the ability to make marketing, accounting and every other area see their relevance and how they fit. (Robbins, 344)

Emotional Intelligence and Leadership Effectiveness

Intelligence or IQ is important to success, but in effect, IQ is simply an example of minimum requirements or skills for the job. It is usually demonstrated through the attainment of degrees or certifications as a baseline for minimum requirements. IQ and technical skills are necessary, but they do not predict who will rise up to be the leader. The best indicator to predict who will emerge as an informal or formal leader is the person with the highest Emotional Quotient or EQ. Possessing and demonstrating the five components of EQ are essential requirements for leadership success.

EQ Components for Leadership

1. **Self—awareness**—Exhibited by self-confidence, realistic self-assessment, and self-deprecating humor.
2. **Self-management**—Exhibited by trustworthiness and integrity, comfort with ambiguity, and openness to change.

3. **Self-motivation**—Exhibited by a strong drive to achieve, optimism, and high organizational commitment.

4. **Empathy**—Exhibited by expertise in building and retaining talent, cross-cultural sensitivity and service to clients and customers.

5. **Social Skills**—Exhibited by the ability to lead change, persuasiveness and expertise in building and leading teams. (Robbins, 346.)

"Leadership isn't about how smart you are, how skilled you are or how high your grades are, it's about understanding what it is to be an emotional human being."

Leadership Theories

There are many different theories on leadership. **Trait Theories,** which try to focus on the traits of leaders and then correlate those traits to successful leadership were popular early on and are finding resurgence in the last twenty years. The problem with Trait Theory was that traits were not universally attributed to effective leaders. Some had these traits and others didn't, yet leadership success still happened.

This spawned the idea that **Behavior Theories** may shed more light on the matter of identifying and predicting leadership if researchers could identify leadership behavior. The implications of this would mean that leaders could be taught to use certain behaviors and therefore could be trained to be leaders. Leadership would be abundant and leaders could be made. However, if Trait Theory proved true, then leaders were born, not made. To the dismay of Behavior Theorists their theories proved somewhat unreliable and had moderate success at best. The question as to whether or not leaders are born or are made is still under debate. It's the same question as nature or nurture. There is probably some validity in both ideas, but it has proven elusive to researchers in identifying the tangibles of leadership, putting them in a box and selling them as a product.

> *"Leadership is an abstract and an intangible that when you see it you know it is present, and equally, when you don't see it, you know it is absent."*

What researchers discovered was that situations and environmental factors were critical to the success or failure of a leader in any given situation. This invoked the idea of **Contingency Theories**. It is the idea that a leader has to be in the right place at the right time with the right skills, abilities, knowledge, and traits to find success. For example, if Martin Luther King Jr. were born in the early1800's, would he have been a civil rights leader even if everything else were the same? The answer is most likely, "no." The environment wasn't conducive to that type of change. Timing, skill, and readiness of those willing to be lead have to be aligned.

> *"The stage on which leadership performs is dynamic, robust and in flux, and then in a moment's notice, the demand for simplicity, generality and stillness are called to center stage and the leader must rewrite the script on the fly."*

Leaders understand that no prescribed way is always the right way. Circumstances outside of one's control often dictate which set of skills or which leadership style may function most effectively. Effective leaders strive to adapt their style based on circumstances.

> *"It is like the fluidity of water, not the rigidness of stone that a leader adapts, bends, flexes and gets creative to overcome the next obstacle."*

Drew Dudley, the Former Leadership Development Coordinator at the University of Toronto, and current CEO of Nuance Leadership Development Services believes that leadership is within us all every day and that we just need to change the way we define leadership.

> *"Leadership is not a characteristic reserved for the extraordinary."*
> (Drew Dudley)

He believes that leadership is something we are all capable of but that we have attributed extraordinary abilities to those who exhibit leadership of incredible proportions, thereby putting "leadership" out of our grasps.

> *"You have made someone's life better by something you said or did. If you think you haven't you are just one of the people that haven't been told. It's scary to think of ourselves as that powerful, it can be frightening that we can matter that much to people, as long as we keep leadership bigger than us, something beyond us, as long as we make it about changing the world, we give ourselves an excuse not to expect it every day, from ourselves and each other."*
> (Drew Dudley)

Drew Dudley—*"Everyday Leadership"*
http://www.ted.com/talks/lang/en/drew_dudley_everyday_leadership.html

> *"Tell the person that made your life better how they affected you. The act of sharing that information is leadership."*

Leadership Types

To understand the various types of leaders and the way they view the world, it is important to understand the situations in which these styles can be most effective. These are very broad and cannot be laid over a group of people, situation or environment like a blanket and expect everyone to be warm and fuzzy. They are guidelines.

Autocratic Leaders—make all decisions and then tell employees what must be done and how to do it. An autocratic style of leadership is generally needed to stimulate unskilled, unmotivated employees. It is good when circumstances require a quick decision, when time is of the essence. In modern management practice it is not a favorable approach. Think small doses.

Democratic Leaders—involve their employees in decisions. The manager presents a situation and encourages his or her subordinates to express opinions and contribute ideas. Highly skilled, trained and motivated employees may respond better to democratic leaders. **Free-Rein Leaders**—let their employees work without much interference. The managers set performance standards and allow employees to find their own ways to meet them. For this style to be effective, employees must know what the standards are, and they must be motivated to attain the standards. The free-rein style of leadership can be a powerful motivator because it demonstrates a great deal of trust and confidence in the employee. Highly skilled, trained and motivated employees may respond better to this style. Democratic and free-rein are leadership styles that reflect the change in the workforce from labor to knowledge workers as discussed in Diversity and the Changing Management Paradigm.

An Example of Situational Blending of Leadership Styles

Let's imagine you are a **Free-Rein** leader and your team is highly effective. They value their autonomy and are glad to use you as a resource for problems they struggle with. Then one day a group comes to you and, after speaking with them, you realize that they have taken serious short cuts in patient care and have missed the valuable point that specific documentation must occur for the doctor and other care providers to be on the same page. Because of this misguided efficiency tactic your staff has taken, a patient has been given a double dose of high level pain medication and intervention is required.

As a **Free-Rein** leader, your natural instinct is to tell them to fix it and report back once it is handled. Would this be effective leadership? Probably not. There is a crisis. You gave them autonomy and they took it to a place that has caused harm to a patient, albeit not intentional, yet they overlooked some basic measures of safety and failed to understand the point of doing it correctly. Their priorities became misaligned with the goals of the organization which are to provide excellent patient care. As the leader, you should engage the problem, understand it, and correct it immediately. There isn't time to talk about it, it needs corrected now. Step one: mitigate any further problems and Step two: illustrate the importance of not repeating this "efficiency shortcut."

The leader should intervene and immediately take corrective action to right the course of the ship which is to realign the goals of the organization with the work of the staff. This is done through **Autocratic Leadership**—tell people what to do and how to do it. Employees should not be demeaned or made to feel as if they were malicious or stupid but the issue needs to be discussed. It isn't a finger pointing session; it is an opportunity for you as the leader to demonstrate quality leadership.

Once you've corrected the issue, and asked them how they arrived at that patient care decision, determine where they veered from the mission, explain why they veered and explain why the correct path is different. Invoke the **Democratic Leadership Style** because your spur of the moment decision may not have been the best decision, but it was necessary at the time to stop the ship from drifting further off course. Ask your employees if they have any better ideas than what you came up with and make sure to align the suggested goals with organizational goals. Remember, if employees have say in a decision, they will buy-in to it and own it.

> *"Just like a nurse uses different gauge needles for different situations, a leader uses different approaches for different situations."*

Leadership Characteristics

After all the research that has been done, and all the top ten lists of leadership qualities, traits and characteristics, there still seems to be no firm and agreed upon list. With that said, there certainly is no prescribed step-by-step process that will ensure you become an effective leader. However, there was a book written by the Chairman and CEO of Tom Peters Group/Learning Systems, James Kouzes and the Dean of the Leavey School of Business and Administration at Santa Clara University, Barry Posner, called *The Leadership Challenge.* In this award winning and influential book, they identified through analyzing thousands of cases and surveys, ten common and fundamental leadership commitments. The key is to understand these and put them to practice. You must be honest with yourself. Do you do these things?

Ten Fundamental Leadership Commitments

<u>**Challenging the Process**</u>
1. ***Search for opportunities***—to change the status quo. Look for innovative ways to improve the organization.
2. ***Experiment and take risks***—since risk taking involves mistakes and failure, leaders accept the inevitable disappointments as learning opportunities.

<u>**Inspire a shared vision**</u>
3. ***Envision an uplifting and ennobling future***
4. ***Enlist others in a common vision***—by appealing to their values, interests, hopes and dreams.

<u>**Enabling Others to Act**</u>
5. ***Foster collaboration***—by promoting cooperative goals and building trust.
6. ***Strengthen people***—by giving power away, providing choice, developing competence, assigning critical tasks, and offering visible support.

<u>**Modeling the Way**</u>
7. ***Set the example***—by behaving in ways that are consistent with shared values.
8. ***Achieve small wins***—that promote consistent progress and build commitment.

<u>**Encouraging the Heart**</u>
9. ***Recognize individual contributions***—to the success of every project.
10. ***Celebrate team accomplishments***—regularly.

(Kousez and Posner, 18)

Characteristics Constituents Admire in Leaders

A study was done by Kouzes and Posner and it asked thousands of people from four continents, (most from the US), to "Select the seven qualities that you most look for and admire in a leader, someone whose direction you would willingly follow." The results follow.

Characteristics	% Choosing	Characteristics	% Choosing
Honest	88	Courageous	29
Forward Looking	75	Cooperative	28
Inspiring	68	Imaginative	28
Competent	63	Caring	23
Fair-Minded	49	Determined	17
Supportive	41	Mature	13
Broad Minded	40	Ambitious	13
Intelligent	40	Loyal	11
Straightforward	33	Self-Controlled	5
Dependable	32	Independent	5

As you will notice from the above list, the characteristics that employees, (and people who are being asked to follow leaders) look for are generally in-line with the Ten Fundamental Leadership Commitments. However, they are not exactly in-line. There is always variation between the lists of traits, qualities and characteristics successful leaders possess. But that is academia for you. This of course lends itself to the enigmatic, intangible and abstract myths surrounding leadership. What we believe to be good leadership skills may be in some situations but not in others. What leaders feel to be strong and just qualities in themselves may not be viewed similarly in the eyes of their followers. It is critical for leaders to be tuned-in, have their finger on the pulse of their constituents and constantly feel around for clues as to the collective mind set of the group.

There will also be informal leaders that influence the group of constituents and these people are key players in the formal and informal attitudes of the group. A good leader knows who those people are and finds ways to enlist them into the value system, goal orientation and structure of the group to not only the group's benefit, but the leader's benefit as well. Remember, the group and the leader live and die together.

> *"Leadership is understanding the needs of the people*
> *you are trying to lead and then give them what they need."*

Clearly from Kouzes and Posner's list above, there are many leadership traits valued by those asked to follow. These various traits or "needs" will rear their heads in various situations. **Emotional Intelligence,** or the ability to engage and have meaningful relationships with others, again comes pouring back to the forefront of the leadership discussion.

> *"It is through Emotional Intelligence that leaders are able to*
> *adapt, understand, empathize and react to the changing needs*
> *of their constituents. People are from different backgrounds;*
> *socio-economic, education, familial, race, gender and religious.*
> *With these differences, people have varying values, ideas of*
> *justice, and needs. You, as the leader need to be tuned in to*
> *perceive their needs (or just ask what they are) and provide the*
> *guidance or ear **they** need, not what **you** think they need."*

Famous Leadership Quotes as Related to Kousez and Posner's Ten Fundamental Leadership Commitments

Let's look now at how influential people over the millennia have viewed leadership and see how their ideas fit into the modern-day Ten Fundamental Leadership Commitments of Kouzes and Posner.

> *"Leadership means seeing and understanding that things can*
> *be bigger than yourself."*

<u>Challenge the Process</u>

1. **Search for Change Opportunities**

   Harry S. Truman—US President—1945-1953

"Men make history and not the other way around. In periods where there is no leadership, society stands still. Progress occurs when courageous, skillful leaders seize the opportunity to change things for the better."

Susan Jeffers—Unknown
"Knowing that we can make a difference in this world is a great motivator. How can we know this and not be involved?"

2. Experiment and Take Risks

Russell H. Ewing—Unknown
"A boss creates fear, a leader confidence. A boss fixes blame, a leader corrects mistakes. A boss knows all, a leader asks questions. A boss makes work drudgery, a leader makes it interesting. A boss is interested in himself or herself, a leader is interested in the group."

George Patton—1912 Olympian (Pentathlon) and Lieutenant General US Military
"Don't tell people how to do things, tell them what to do and let them surprise you with their results."

Inspire a Shared Vision

3. Envision the Future

Woodrow Wilson—US President—1913-1921
"Absolute identity with one's cause is the first and great condition of successful leadership."

Theodore M. Hesburgh—President of The University of Notre Dame 1952-1987
"The very essence of leadership is that you must have vision. You can't blow an uncertain trumpet."

Proverbs 29:18—God—known as the creator of all things
"Where there is no vision, the people perish."

4. Enlist Others in a Common Vision

Lao Tzu—5ᵗʰ-4ᵗʰ Century BC Chinese Philosopher, known as founder of Taoism
"Go to the people. Learn from them. Live with them. Start with what they know. Build with what they have. The best of leaders, when the job is done, when the task is accomplished, the people will say we have done it ourselves."

Nelson Mandela—South African President and Anti-Apartheid Activist
"It is better to lead from behind and to put others in front, especially when you celebrate victory when nice things occur. You take the front-line when there is danger. Then people will appreciate your leadership."

Enable Others to Act

5. Foster Collaboration

Mahatma Gandhi (Great Soul)—Led India to Independence through Non-Violent Civil Disobedience
"I suppose leadership at one time meant muscles; but today it means getting along with people."

Dwight D. Eisenhower—US President 1953-1961
"Leadership is the art of getting someone else to do something you want done because he wants to do it."

Henry Gilmer—Unknown
"Look over your shoulder now and then to be sure someone's following you."

6. Strengthen People

John Quincy Adams—US President 1825-1829
"If your actions inspire others to dream more, learn more, do more and become more, you are a leader."

Jim Rohn—Author, Entrepreneur 1930-2009
"A good objective of leadership is to help those who are doing poorly to do well and to help those who are doing well to do even better."

Dwight D. Eisenhower—US President 1953-1961
"You don't lead by hitting people over the head—that's assault, not leadership."

John D. Rockefeller—Oil Industrialist & Philanthropist 1839-1937
"Good leadership consists of showing average people how to do the work of superior people."

Rosalynn Carter—First Lady of the US 1977-1981
"A leader takes people where they want to go. A great leader takes people where they don't necessarily want to go, but ought to be."

Model the Way

7. Set the Example

Barack Obama—US President 2008-present
"We can't drive our SUVs and eat as much as we want and keep our homes on 72 degrees at all times . . . and then just expect that other countries are going to say OK. That's not leadership. That's not going to happen."

Albert Schweitzer—Theologin, Organist, Philosopher, Physician, Medical Missionary 1875-1965
"Example is leadership."

Robert Half—Founder of Robert Half International, S&P 500
"Delegating work, works, provided the one delegating works, too."

8. Achieve Small Wins

Patrick Lencioni—Author and Business Consultant
"As a leader, you're probably not doing a good job unless your employees can do a good impression of you when you're not around."

Margaret Mead—Cultural Anthropologist 1901-1978
*"Never doubt that a small group of thoughtful committed citizens can change the world.
Indeed, it is the only thing that ever has."*

Carly Fiorina, CEO Hewlett Packard 1999-2005
"Leadership comes in small acts as well as bold strokes."

Encourage the Heart

9. Recognize Individuals

Max DePree—CEO Herman Miller Furniture/Author
*"The first responsibility of a leader is to define reality.
The last is to say thank you.
In between, the leader is a servant."*

Rosabeth Moss Kantor—Tenured Harvard Business Professor
"Leaders are more powerful role models when they learn than when they teach."

Arnold H. Glasgow - Unknown
"A good leader takes a little more than his share of the blame, a little less than his share of the credit."

10. Celebrate

Robert Burton—1577-1640 English Scholar
"I light my candle from their torches."

Ovid (Publius Ovidius Naso) Roman Poet 43BC—17AD
"A ruler should be slow to punish and swift to reward."

These quotes cover a large span of time and culture. After reviewing them, one thing is abundantly clear, leadership is a concept like love that people view and feel universally. Like love, we can only speak about it in metaphor, analogy, narrative, and what it isn't. Like love, leadership is felt and exhibited through sincerity, honesty, integrity, compassion, visions of the future and collaboration with others when one realizes that things may just be larger than themselves. Leadership is like love in that it isn't something you can touch, see, or taste, but you know when it arrives and you know when it leaves. To try to express love or leadership in words, one falls short. The only way to illustrate either effectively is to demonstrate the intangible qualities of each through your actions and simply do it! Try! And if you fail, learn from it. If you learn, you are successful and you've taken the first and most important step toward becoming a better leader.

Chapter 4—Motivation

Overview on Motivation

*"A creative man is motivated by the desire to achieve,
not by the desire to beat others."* (Ayn Rand)

*"I do not try to dance better than anyone else,
I only try to dance better than myself."* (Mikhail Baryshnikov)

For the most part, we can thank motivation for all the wonderful creations, innovations, and good in the world, not to mention the perpetuation of human beings. Most of the incredible things we have or enjoy are derived from the desire to make things better not only for ourselves but for others and, specifically, the greater good. When people do things with the right motivation, magnificent things result. **Motivation** is an inner drive that directs a person's behavior toward goals. A **goal** is the satisfaction of a need, and a **need** is the difference between a desired state and an actual state.

Of course, motivation can also wreak havoc if it is from a place of suboptimum balance, such as the desire to dominate, gain power, or to receive accolades for performing well. This motivation created the atomic bomb, the nuclear bomb, unethical behavior and is also responsible for those people in the workplace who just can't seem to find peace in their work or with the work of others. No matter what, they find something wrong with their environment, the work itself or the people around them; it's because they just can't seem to be positive. They errantly feel that they are in need of external factors to satisfy the discrepancy between what they need internally and what they are getting and what they desire externally and what they get. These two main types of motivation are intrinsic and extrinsic.

Intrinsic Motivation calls people to action from an internal need to fulfill some outcome for personal satisfaction such as being all they can be, and helping another person from a place of benevolence. It is a desire to be effective and to perform a behavior for its own sake, (Myers, 473) because they enjoy it and gain satisfaction from it. This is deep satisfaction and long lasting.

"Intrinsic motivation provides a satisfaction that propels people, feeds their soul and sustains their inner ambition and drive."

Extrinsic Motivation—calls people to action from an external need to fulfill some outcome, such as money, power, prestige or notoriety. It is seeking external rewards and avoiding punishments. (Myers, 473) It is a desire to be noticed, to gain attention or obtain material objects.

"Extrinsic Motivation provides fleeting satisfaction that ultimately leaves one feeling empty and striving to fill an ever increasing and insatiable desire for more."

When a person does something because they expect some external validation or reward they are selling themselves short and will never reach self-actualization as Maslow describes it. They sell themselves short because they are not doing what they need to do to fulfill their own internal needs and desires for satisfaction. They fall short because no external validation or reward can surpass or supplant the satisfaction that is derived from doing something because it is what one simply has to do, for themselves.

"It is difficult to take care of others and to be liked by others, when one does not take care of and like themselves."

A study done by Janet Spence and Robert Helmreich in 1983 concluded that intrinsic motivation produces high achievement and that extrinsic motivation (such as the desire for a high paying career) often does not. Spence and Helmreich identified and assessed three facets of motivation:

1. **People's quests for mastery**—as shown, for example, by their strongly agreeing that, "if I am not good at something I would rather keep struggling to master it than move on to something I may be good at."—<u>Intrinsic</u>
2. **Their drive to work**—"I like to work hard."—<u>Intrinsic</u>
3. **Their competitiveness** "I really enjoy working in situations involving skill and competition."—<u>Extrinsic</u>

> *"Despite similar abilities, people oriented toward mastery and hard work typically achieve more. If students, they get better grades; if MBA graduates, they earn more money: if scientists, their work is more often cited by other scientists. No surprise there. But, surprisingly in Spence and Helmreich's studies those who were most competitive (which is a more extrinsic orientation) often achieved less." (Myers, 373)*

Employee motivation effects productivity, and part of a manager's job is to channel motivation toward the accomplishment of organizational goals. The study of motivation helps managers understand what prompts people to initiate action, what influences their choice of action and why they persist in that action over time. (Daft, Marcic, 410) It not only affects productivity but it affects how they perceive their environment, their morale, and their confidence and resolve to do what is right.

As leaders we want people who are "in it" for the right reasons. We want nurses who are called to nursing, not to the money, and we want doctors who have an immense desire to cure and make life better, rather than seek the prestige that comes from being a doctor.

For leaders to surround themselves with people who are intrinsically motivated is a tremendous step toward success. However, this is not exactly practical. So, what we are left with as leaders is a need to understand what motivates people. The following pages will describe various theories of motivation and shed light on the reasons people feel motivated, and the reasons they feel unmotivated.

11 Perspectives on Motivational Theory and Work

1. **Goal Setting Theory** is a motivational theory which states that people have conscious goals that energize them and direct their thoughts and behaviors toward one end. (Bateman, Snell, 413) People can use goals to guide their behavior and steer them to a mutually rewarding end for the organization and themselves. To do this there are a few factors that must be in place for goals to be effective:

> A.   **The goal must be acceptable to the employee**—goals must not conflict with the employee's values and there should be a reason for the person to pursue those goals. Mutual goal development is a key component to developing acceptable goals that people want to strive for. Goals are much more effective if the person trying to reach the goal has helped develop the goal rather than that goal being handed to them by someone else;
>
> B.   **Challenging but attainable**—goals should push and inspire people to improve performance but, as we'll learn later with the expectancy theory of motivation, if the expectation of attaining the goal is unrealistic, motivation suffers significantly and can even work against the attainment of goals;
>
> C.   **Specific, quantifiable, and measurable**—if an employee can see that they have reached their goal, the feeling of satisfaction is greater. The attainment of a goal should be finite and definitive. It is like painting a wall and stepping back, nodding your head and saying, "That looks good. I did a good job." It helps to know when success has been attained or when it is still pending. Ambiguity leads to uncertainty and uncertainty leads to assumptions and assumptions lead to negativity.

"Reaching a goal is validation for hard work and inspiration to go after the next goal."

Goals and plans help employees identify with the organization and motivate them by reducing uncertainty and clarifying **what** should be accomplished. Lack of a clear goal can damage employee motivation and commitment. Whereas a goal provides the **why** of an organization or subunit's existence, a plan tells the **how.** (Daft, Marcic, 140) Each functional unit of an organization can develop their own goals so employees can understand why they are doing what they are doing.

It is even advisable to develop these goals and plans as a group. Identify the "why", "how" and "what," of what you do. These can act as guide posts for you and your employees to help keep everyone on track and focused. It will also establish what you believe as a group and it will allow each person to monitor their behavior as it relates to reaching the goal.

The Golden Circle as Related to Goal Setting and Motivation

Simon Sinek works for the RAND Corporation as an adjunct staff member and advises on matters of military innovation and planning. The video below is the 7th most frequently viewed video on TEDTV.com with nearly 7.5 million views.

Simon Sinek: *"How Great Leaders Inspire Action"* http://www. ted.com/talks/simon_sinek_how_great_leaders_inspire_action. html?source=email#.T5Wc3b4ulWh.email

Simon Sinek describes *"How Great Leaders Inspire Action,"* in terms of the Golden Circle as the following illustration describes. It is a simple concept, but very powerful. For one, if we "answer the why," as we discussed in the section on communication, we are answering the very reason for initiating action in the first place. If you, as a leader can speak to people at this level, and get them to believe in "why" they do what they do, the "how" and the "what" just happen. It is when a person doesn't have a firm grasp as to "why" they do something that they lack the proper motivation to do it. If that motivation comes from within, or is intrinsic in nature, the likelihood of success will be greater because they are doing it for themselves, not for someone else.

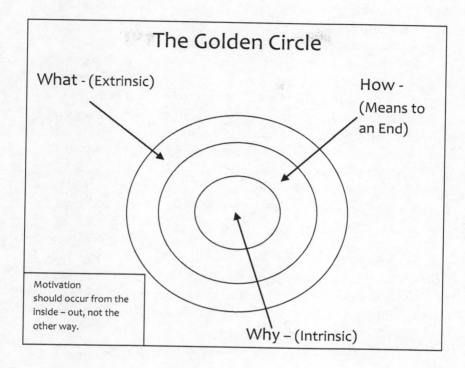

As an example, if an Emergency Room wanted to sit down and hash out the "why", "how" and "what" of their work, it may look something like this.

Why
"We believe in giving everyone in need efficient, and effective emergency care in an attempt to heal and save lives."
How
"We treat every person as our primary concern."
What
"We provide lifesaving services to our community, friends and family."

Often we tell people "what" they need to do and "how" they need to do it, but we forget to explain "why" they need to do it. Take for example nursing, we understand "what" needs to be done—take care of patients, and we understand "how" to take care of patients, (RN's learned this in school) but the gap often comes when we can't agree on "why" we take care of patients. Some nurses are called to nursing because they want to take care of people and they find personal satisfaction in making the lives of others better or less painful. The act of caring for others is all the motivation they need and they derive satisfaction and need fulfillment from the act itself. The "how" and "what" are secondary. The desire to be a nurse is from an intrinsic place of motivation.

On the other hand, there are nurses that find their motivation to be a nurse from extrinsic sources of motivation, such as money, prestige, or a favorable schedule. They go to school and learn "what" nursing is and "how" to be a nurse through orientation, and then the "why" of being a nurse is lost or misaligned with other nurses that desire to be a nurse because of intrinsic motivation. This incongruous motivation causes problems. The belief systems that these two groups operate under are at opposite ends of the spectrum.

> *"If you hire people just because they can do a job,*
> *they'll work for your money.*
> *But if you hire people who believe what you believe,*
> *they'll work for you with blood and sweat and tears."*
> (Simon Sinek)

The key to developing a team that is motivated by the proper "why," is to hire people who are motivated intrinsically, people who find their reward in helping patients and making them better, not for money, not for working hours and not for prestige.

> *"Motivation should flow from the inside (intrinsically)*
> *to the outside (extrinsically), not the opposite."*

2. Classical Theory of Motivation—Money is the sole motivator for workers. Fredrick Taylor believed that productivity was related to financial incentive. He suggested that workers who were paid more would produce more. Time and time again, and study after study has proven this theory inaccurate.

"Money isn't the most powerful motivator."

3. Hawthorne Studies—in 1924, Elton Mayo and his colleagues from Harvard University tried to link physical conditions to productivity. They wanted to look at things such as light and noise levels in the work environment. What they discovered was no matter what the physical changes to the environment were, productivity increased. This was not the expected result. What they discovered through interviews with the employees involved in the study was that the employees expressed satisfaction not only because their co-workers were friendly, but because their supervisors had asked for their help and input in the study. To state this in simpler terms, the researchers found that employees were not responding to the change in physical conditions, they were responding positively to the attention they received from management and researchers. Elton Mayo and his colleagues concluded that social and psychological factors could significantly affect productivity, satisfaction and morale.

The Hawthorne studies opened the door to the idea that human relations influence employees and productivity. It was concluded that managers who attend to the needs, beliefs, and expectations of their people, will have more success when trying to motivate employees.

"Taking an interest and showing you care is a powerful motivator."

4. Maslow's Needs Hierarchy of Motivation—This theory illustrates the five basic needs people have and the order in which they strive to reach them. One may not skip over a lower level need to a higher level need without obtaining them in sequential order. Satisfaction must be obtained in the lower level need before one can move to a higher level need. Our interest is in understanding how leaders can align work with the attainment of higher order needs.

"A person who is cold and starving is not going to worry about respect from his or her colleagues until he or she is warm and hunger is satiated."

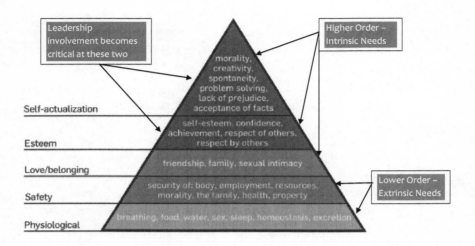

1ˢᵗ Level Needs—Physiological Needs
(Extrinsic)—Obtaining employment will provide shelter and food. It will also make the potential for sex more likely, but of course that will still need to be handled outside of work.

2ⁿᵈ Level Needs—Safety and Security
(Extrinsic)—Employment will provide a means to maintaining food and shelter on an on-going basis, and the result is the safety need is satisfied.

3ʳᵈ Level Needs—Social (Intrinsic)—Employment will
provide a venue to develop social relationships, teams, and acceptance from others. This is the first stage in attaining higher order needs that come from intrinsic motivation rather than extrinsic motivation.

4ᵗʰ Level Needs—Self-Esteem (Intrinsic)—This is
where leadership can get involved and really make

employment a worthwhile venture for both the employee and the organization. Self-esteem can be obtained through the development of mutually respectful and valuable relationships. An organization should not hire an employee unless the organization can truly value and respect the employee's contributions. Leaders can get more from employees if they can recognize the employee's contributions and acknowledge them in a meaningful way. By doing so, the manager is assisting the employee with one of the higher order needs and producing a higher functioning person who feels good about themselves and their work.

5th Level Needs—Self—Actualization

(Intrinsic)—Concerning employment, if leaders encourage employees and assist them in obtaining this need, the sky is the limit. We want employees to open their wings and soar. This is the most dynamic aspect of the employment relationship. Once the employee has attained the lower order needs, they will desire to maximize their full-potential. This is also the place where a leader can reap the most reward as well. A leader's goal should be to help each employee be the best they can be. Of course, this will require effort and interest from the employee and encouragement and commitment from the leader and the organization. The concept is simple, if a leader can keep as many employees as possible striving for self-actualization, reaching it, and moving on to the next challenge, it becomes a win/win for both the employee and organization. The organization will have a long-term engaged employee and the employee will constantly be striving to become self-actualized while fulfilling intrinsic needs.

5. Douglas McGregor's Theory X—(The Negative) McGregor sorted through all the different management approaches, ideas and viewpoints and distilled them down to a very common derivative—positive and negative approaches.

Theory X managers believe that:

A. Employees do not want to work
B. Employees dislike work and will try to avoid work
C. Employees need to be coerced to work, must be strictly controlled and threatened to achieve organizational goals.
D. Employees prefer to be directed and do not like to make decisions. They avoid responsibility and have little ambition for achievement.

This style of management lends itself to a culture of fear and intimidation, micro-management, and very little creativity and innovation. These managers often think no one can do the job as well as they could, so they prescribe very tight controls over their employees. They ask for little or no input from their employees and make decisions in an autocratic style as discussed in the last chapter. This type of manager does not consider that employees may be able to obtain social, self-esteem and self-actualization needs through work, because they believe employees are only working as a means to food, shelter, and security.

6. **Douglas McGregor's Theory Y—(The Positive)** This approach is a more humanistic approach toward work. Managers who subscribe to this style believe employees want to do a good job, and that they will strive to attain social, esteem and even self-actualization needs if given the proper environment and conditions.

McGregor describes the assumptions behind Theory Y in the following way:

A. The expenditure of physical and mental effort in work is as natural as play or rest.
B. People will exercise self-direction and self-control to achieve objectives to which they are committed.

C. People will commit to objectives when they realize that the achievement of those goals will bring them internal, personal reward.

D. The average person will seek and accept responsibility.

E. Imagination, ingenuity and creativity can help solve organizational problems.

F. Organizations today do not make full use of worker's intellectual potential.

"Theory X and Y are the self-fulfilling prophecy in action.
If you believe an employee is good or bad,
they'll respond by being either a good or bad employee."

7. Equity Theory

Equity theory purports the assumption that how much a person is willing to give an organization is dependent on the reward they will receive for their efforts.

If for example, an employee believes that their efforts or the amount of work they are asked to perform are more valuable to the organization than the reward they expect to receive, they will only perform the amount of work they feel is equal to the reward they will receive. Often an employee will compare their input in skill, experience, and effort and assess how that compares to the output, or reward of other people. If they feel their input and output is similar to that of others, or in proportion they feel there is equity. If there isn't equity, they work to create equity by asking to increase their output, in the form of pay, or by decreasing their peers output by trying to have co-workers paid less or by just doing less to balance the scales of justice. If there is inequity in an employee's perception of the input and output, they will most likely look for another job that can provide a sense of equity. This can manifest itself intrinsically and extrinsically.

"What an employee is getting from an employer,
must equal what the employee feels they are giving.

> *If it is perceived to be out of balance, the employee*
> *will actively work to balance it."*

8. Expectancy Theory

States that the more likely a person is to obtain a certain reward, the more motivated they will be to obtain it. If the likelihood of obtaining a reward is scarce, then the motivation will not be strong.

"People won't even try to attain an unrealistic goal and in fact, may sabotage it to prove just how unrealistic it is."

9. Two-Factor Theory of Motivation—(or sometimes referred to as Motivation-Hygiene Theory) Frederick Herzberg developed this theory of motivation called the Two Factor Theory. It distinguishes between two factors, hygiene and motivators.

A. "Hygiene factors—(Extrinsic)—involve the presence or absence of job dissatisfiers, including working conditions, pay, company policies and interpersonal relationships." (Daft, Marcic, 415)

If these factors are absent, employees feel dissatisfied with their work, however if they are present, the dissatisfaction is removed, but they do not become highly satisfied, or motivated to excel. These are the extrinsic motivators, and as you can see, they only remove dissatisfaction, they do not create satisfaction. These are similar to the lower order needs in Maslow's Needs Hierarchy—physiological and safety needs.

B. "Motivation factors—(Intrinsic)—influence job satisfaction based on fulfillment of high-level needs such as achievement, recognition, responsibility and opportunity for growth. (Daft, Marcic, 415)

When these factors are not present, employees feel neutral toward work, but if they are present, they feel motivated to perform at higher levels and become satisfied. These are the intrinsic motivators, and if they are fulfilled, employees will likely be satisfied. They are similar to the higher order needs that Maslow described; social, self-esteem, and self-actualization.

For the hygiene theory to actually motivate employees and make them fully satisfied, it requires the two parts of the system operate in conjunction with the other for success. If one is present and the other isn't, the outcome is the same, a neutral feeling toward work. For the Two Factor Theory to be successful both hygiene factors and motivational factors must be present.

As this relates to Maslow's Needs Hierarchy, if employees are struggling to find the right equipment because there isn't enough, and they are stretched too thin personnel wise, they effectively are huddled in a corner freezing and starving. They are trying to obtain the basic needs of food, shelter, water and safety. Yet, so often we ask them to be social, engage the patient, smile and improve self-esteem and ultimately be all they can be and find self-actualization. Simply put if the hygiene factors are not present there is no reason to even talk about motivators. They are just trying to survive. This is why customer and patient satisfaction suffers, yet we too often do not want to admit that we have set everyone up for misery and a day spent just trying to get by. The need or desire for more, more, more and more growth from industry is a principle concern when it comes to the well-being of our future's worker. Growth is not infinite and at some point too much growth and diminishing resources means we have to eat ourselves.

10. **Reinforcement Perspective of Motivation** advocates the appropriate use of rewards and punishments to modify behaviors. The goal of reinforcement theory is to encourage or deter certain behaviors. Behavior modification is the goal and this is carried out on the assumption that behavior that is positively reinforced will be repeated and behavior that is not reinforced will not be repeated.

There are four reinforcement tools available to change human behavior:

A. **Positive Reinforcement**—to actively give pleasant and positive feedback for desired behavior whether in verbal, financial, or other forms. For example, when you see someone doing what they should, tell them, "good job." This will encourage the behavior to continue. Ambiguity is the enemy.

B. **Avoidance Learning**—is producing a desired outcome so negative consequences will cease. For example, if an employee stops a certain behavior, the supervisor will stop nagging them about it.

C. **Punishment**—is to subject unpleasant consequences on someone for undesired behavior. This is not exactly a favorable way to motivate people, due to the fact it fails to explain the correct way to behave, and is often demeaning. It could also create fear and intimidation.

D. **Extinction**—if a behavior is not rewarded the behavior will cease to exist or become extinct. For example, if an employee fails to receive raises because they are short and nasty to co-workers, they may stop being short and nasty in order to have the reward of increases reinstated.

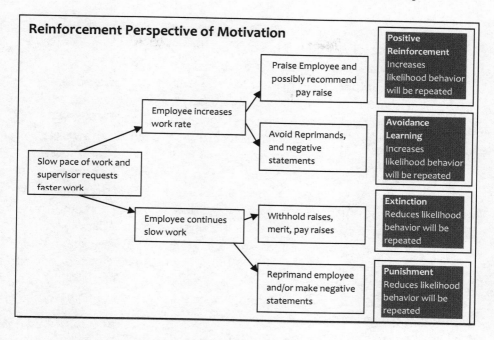

Reinforcement Perspective of Motivation

It is through the **Law of Effect** that these principles come to light. The Law of Effect states that positive reinforcement encourages continued, desirable behavior, and negatively reinforced behavior inhibits the continuation of undesirable behavior. It is a more desirable approach to positively reinforce behavior rather than to negatively reinforce behavior. Learning organizations want employees to grow and feel good about their work, not fear the outcomes of poor work. Again, it is the difference between developing a culture of fear and intimidation, and one of mutual respect and growth.

*"Fear creates anger, anger creates hatred and
hatred creates suffering."* (Yoda)

11. **Empowerment as a motivator**—this is a process of sharing power with employees, thereby enhancing confidence in their ability to perform their jobs and their belief that they are influential contributors to the organization. (Bateman, Snell, 425)

It is a very powerful way to illustrate to an employee that they are valuable, capable, and qualified to do the job they have been hired for. It is also a powerful way to get people to buy-in to goal attainment. Often though, manager's say, "You are empowered to do what needs done," and then when the employee does what they think to be right, they get an ear full from the manager who says, "That's not what I would have done." Managers cannot send mixed messages. They can set parameters, but they cannot undermine decisions. This will make people stagnant and unmotivated. Saying, "I empower you," is a joke. To actually empower someone, the leader needs to make the environment conducive to a real diffusion of power, and put it into the hands of the people who can affect change.

Fostering Empowerment is a process not a grandiose declaration. It happens in action, not words. The following factors are necessary to create an environment of empowerment where everyone feels they have a real influence over performance standards and business effectiveness within their area of responsibility. To do so these factors must be present. (Bateman, Snell, 426)

Tips for Fostering Empowerment

1. **Information**—information must flow freely and must be relevant to the success of the employee.
2. **Knowledge**—employees need to know how to use the information which means they must be adequately oriented and trained to make decisions based on the information and the resources available.
3. **Power**—must be given adequately so that employees can take the information they are given, the knowledge they have gained and make decisions that give them proper control over their work to succeed.
4. **Rewards**—upon success, rewards must be given to the employee. The rewards that come from empowerment are often *intrinsic* in nature and come in the form of a sense of accomplishment, control, ownership and buy-in to their work-life. To close the loop of empowerment secondary rewards or *extrinsic* rewards such as a thank you note, pat

on the back, public recognition or even a small token of appreciation are useful tools.

> *"If a leader isn't confident in the people they've hired, and can't relinquish power to the people they've put in place to make things work, it usually isn't the employee's fault."*

What's Your Motive?

As a leader, you should be open to the idea that different people see the world differently. We discussed in the first chapter on Diversity and the Changing Management Paradigm, the idea that different generations have different ideas related to work, which also means they are motivated by different drivers. For example, Generation X wants empowerment, innovation, participation, and teamwork. Generation Y values technology, family, and they are confident, crave feedback and want to achieve and be recognized.

Which managerial style is effective varies with the people managed. To motivate people, Martin Maeher and Larry Braskamp advise managers to assess their people's motives and adjust their managerial (or leadership) style accordingly. Challenge employees who value accomplishment to try new things and to exhibit excellence. Give those who value recognition the attention they desire. Place those who value affiliation in a unit that has a trustful family feeling and that shares decision making. Motivate those who value power with competition and opportunities for triumphant success. Different strokes for different folks, but for each a way to energize and direct—in a word, to motivate—behavior. (Myers, 376)

The idea of motivation comes in different forms for different people. A leader's role is to determine what needs an employee desires to have filled and work with them to fulfill those needs (refer to Maslow). The act of concern alone (the Hawthorne Effect) will provide positive results. The identification of employee motivators (intrinsic or extrinsic) will steer you in providing what the employee lacks. The understanding as to how an employee thinks will allow the leader to provide equity and meet expectations of goal attainment, (refer to expectancy and equity theories.)

As a leader, ensure the Hygiene factors are not draining your employees and are at a minimum keeping them primed for increased motivation and satisfaction. This means equipment, resources and the environment need to be satisfactory. Then guide employees and help them reach their self-esteem goals, and ultimately find self-actualization, (refer to Herzberg's Two-Factory Theory/Maslow.)

This is a daunting task, but the investment at the front-end will pay huge dividends at the back-end. Employees will be autonomous, energized and have a positive attitude toward work. Leaders will not have to deal with trite employee grievances, disputes, and misguided negativity. Ultimately, a mutual respect will be attained and the employee and leader will look out for one another and strive to see the other succeed, knowing that one cannot succeed without the other's success. You will have developed teams that push in the same direction, no matter how steep the hill, toward the same objective and after the same goals; (refer to goal-setting theory.)

"Leaders must let their ego, go.
Realize that the success and sense of accomplishment and
control an employee feels is the best gift you can give them.
Leaders motivate by making other's better."

Chapter 5—Organizational Development, Change and Innovation

Overview on Organizational Development, Change and Innovation

As one progresses through their work-life, one thing is absolutely certain, change is a given. Change is like gravity. We know that items fall to earth at the rate of 9.8 meters per second. Just as we trust we will stick to earth, we should also trust that each day, change of some sort will occur. Once we've agreed to this idea, and once we've come to terms with the constant and given nature of change we can embrace it, rather than dread it as if it is some looming and unfortunate surprise.

Just like we naturally embrace the fact that gravity will always be there, pushing on us, we can embrace the idea that change will always be there pushing as well. If so, we have a better likelihood of harnessing the inevitable power of change and directing it for the better.

"Change, just like gravity, is constant—it will always occur."

Imagine if a professional baseball pitcher constantly wondered if when he threw a pitch, gravity would push the ball to earth or that possibly gravity would cease to exist and the ball would just streak into the ether of outer space. The uncertainty of this thought process would cause him to alter his pitch, and leave him wondering if in fact gravity would be there to help him or hurt him. Because of the constant nature of gravity, he trusts that it will be there, consistently working on each pitch every time. The key is that he doesn't question whether or not gravity will affect his pitch; he knows it and uses that force to throw strikes.

If we agree that change is inevitable and constant, we can use it to benefit the people around us, and ourselves as leaders, just like a major league pitcher uses gravity to help him throw strikes. Change is often thought of as a negative, because people sometimes cannot concede to the fact that change is happening whether they like it, fight it or embrace it. Some people like to fight change. Others embrace it and view it as a positive opportunity to learn something and develop a new perspective on an issue or experience.

Some people pretend that change is not happening around them, all the time. People want to act like change isn't occurring if they don't acknowledge it. One could argue that change is uncertain and for some, uncertainty is scary, and as we learned in the last chapter, "Fear creates anger, anger creates hatred and hatred creates suffering." When in fact, change isn't uncertain at all—it happens all the time and always will, just like gravity. The only thing uncertain about change is how it will manifest. What form will change take?

If we can accept the idea that change isn't something to fear; but that change is something we can dictate, control and manipulate, it becomes our friend, and opens the door for improvement, increased satisfaction, and innovation. In fact, all the luxuries and niceties in life are a result of change and more importantly, innovation. If we as leaders can embrace the consistency of change, and encourage our co-workers to accept this, and expect it, the barriers to change, improvement and innovation will lessen.

One can change a process and make things different, or create a completely new and original idea (innovation) that will solve a problem. **Change management** is an approach to shifting/ transitioning individuals, teams and organizations from a current state to a desired future state. It is an organizational process aimed at helping stakeholders accept and embrace changes in their business environment.

General Reasons for Resistance to Change

Even if we as leaders grow to understand that change is inevitable, and something that we can embrace, we are still going to have to understand the obstacles employees and others may have with the change process. Of course understanding what obstacles may be present is the first step in being able to overcome those obstacles. A leader can scan the environment to try to identify which of these obstacles may be present in order to prioritize which may be affecting the change initiative.

1. **Inertia**—Usually people do not want to disturb the status quo. The old ways of doing things are comfortable and easy, so people don't want to shake things up and try something new.
2. **Timing**—People often resist change because of poor timing. If managers or employees are unusually busy or under stress, or if relations between management and workers are strained, the timing is wrong for introducing new proposals. Where possible, leaders should introduce change when people are receptive.
3. **Surprise**—One key aspect of timing and receptivity is surprise. If the change is sudden, unexpected, or extreme, resistance may be the initial, almost reflexive reaction. One must have time to prepare for the change.
4. **Peer pressure**—Sometimes work teams resist new ideas. Even if individual members do not strongly oppose a change suggested by management, the team may band together in opposition. (Bateman Snell, 584)

Just as change is a given, so is the resistance to change. The critical factor is how change is introduced and what skills you have as a leader to overcome resistance and settle on change that is agreeable to the most people. Just as we've discussed in prior chapters, there are positive and negative approaches to everything. We can choose to take an approach that mirrors the ideas and beliefs of a Theory Y manager or we can choose an approach that mimics that of the authoritarian, Theory X manager. A Theory X approach would yield quick change at the front-end, but major issues at the tail-end. Whereas, a Theory Y approach will most likely take time at the beginning of change, but have better, more stable results at the tail-end.

Methods for Dealing with Resistance to Change

Approach	Commonly used in situations	Advantages	Drawbacks
Education and Communication (Positive)	Where there is a lack of information or inaccurate information and analysis.	Once persuaded, people will often help with the implementation of the change.	Can be very time-consuming are involved.
Participation and Involvement (Positive)	Where the initiators do not have all the information they need to design the change, and where others have considerable power to resist.	People who participate will be committed to implementing change, and any relevant information they have will be integrated into the change plan.	Can be time-consuming if participators design an inappropriate change.
Facilitation and and Support (Positive)	Where people are resisting because of adjustment problems.	No other approach works as well with adjustment problems.	Can be time-consuming and expensive, still fail.
Negotiation and Agreement (Neutral)	Where someone or some group will clearly lose out in a change, and where that group has considerable power to resist.	Sometimes it is a relatively easy way to avoid major resistance.	Can be too expensive in many cases if it alerts others to negotiate.
Manipulation and Cooptation (Negative)	Where other tactics will not work, or are too expensive.	It can be a relatively quick and inexpensive solution to resistance problems.	Can lead to future problems if people feel manipulated.

Planned Change Models

Kurt Lewin introduced a Change Theory in the 1940's that was built around *unfreezing* behavior, *moving* behavior and *refreezing* behavior. These three ideas were expanded on by Edgar Schein by applying psychological understanding to each stage. To further understand how the three stage model fits into the idea of Organizational Development we must understand this concept. **Organizational Development** is planned change. As we know, change is constant and is always presenting something new and different to us. With organizational development, we as leaders, first need to identify what needs changed, and then how. Once that has been established we can apply the Three Stage Model for Change. For change to occur a current process, procedure, style or format must become weak or less useful, or have the potential to become weak or less useful. The spark for change is a gap. Change is the result of something faltering or not meeting the expected needs. A **gap** exists between what is needed and what is being received. **Change** is the process of becoming different. Ideally, we want to focus on proactive change rather than reactive change. This will be addressed on the following pages.

"Necessity is the mother of invention." (Unknown origin)
Interpretation
"Difficult situations inspire ingenious solutions."

Time invested at the front-end of a change process is much better spent than at the tail-end of the process.

It is the investment up front in . . .

1. **Employee Input**
2. **Employee Buy-in**
3. **Employee communication about fears, apprehensions, and ideas**

. . . that will reap the most positive and effective results to the change process.

So often in healthcare, leaders identify a problem like poor patient satisfaction and throw a half-cocked gimmick at it and walk away. Leaders do not involve the players who will be responsible for the day-to-day process change to identify obstacles or shortcomings. Often it is because leaders juggle multiple change initiatives and then when they have too many initiatives in the air and become overwhelmed they delegate one or more initiatives to someone else and tell them to implement them. The most alarming part of this strategy is that the leader comes back a month later and expects the change to have taken hold. If it didn't, the leader scrambles to put together another solution and then throws it at the problem again. The worst part is we call this progress, just so we can say we did something, or worse, we look for other reasons why the "change" didn't take root and assign blame. The answer is; we didn't nurture it or water it. We just threw what may have been a viable solution or seed at a dried up field and hoped for the best. We need to prepare the environment and people for change at the front-end.

> *"Invest your effort, energy and time at the front-end of the change process and as change occurs, it will get easier.*

For example, it is similar to the idea of a family moving, and taking a child out of one school and putting them in a new school. You can simply move, have the child wait at the bus stop the first day of school and hope they figure it out in a reasonable amount of time without much anguish. Most likely however, they will run into obstacles, unfamiliar situations, and won't know their way around.

Or . . . you can tell the child that you may be moving, and then when the decision is made, explain to them why it was made and that they will be attending a really good school. Tell the child the reasons why the new school will be better and then take them to it so they can have the mental image of the school in their head and start imagining themselves there. Take them on a tour of the school and let them meet their teacher in advance. You could even let them shadow a selected student for a day and get to know the way things work and maybe meet a few kids that will be in his/her new class.

That investment of time and information at the front-end may well and positively transition your child from his old school to his new school and likely make the situation better because he or she can leave behind the bad stuff. Because you've focused your attention on the front-end of the change, the back end will be smoother.

Or . . . . you can throw the child in the new school without communicating or investing any time, energy, or effort at the front-end and have a disgruntled, disobedient child who acts out and needs thousands of dollars of therapy. It is your call. You are the leader. You are in charge.

Lewin's Three Stage Model for Planned Change

This model describes the cognitive gymnastics people bound through to get to the other side of change. Remember, change starts at point A and ends at point B. The quickest way from one point to another is a straight line. The key is that it may take time to work around the cognitive obstacles that people will inevitably throw in the path of change. Change very rarely ever looks like a straight line. The goal is to minimize the deviations from the path of change.

Stage 1—Unfreezing *(Allowing oneself to consider change)*
The disconfirmation of a process creates pain and discomfort, which cause guilt and anxiety, which motivates the person to change. But unless the person feels comfortable with dropping the old behaviors and acquiring new ones, change will not occur. That is, the person must experience a sense of psychological safety in order to replace the old behaviors with new behaviors. *(Like explaining to your child they will be attending a new school, showing them the new school and touring the new school.)*

Stage 2—Moving *(The person shifts their cognitive paradigm to begin change)*
The person undergoes cognitive restructuring. The person needs information and evidence to show that the change is desirable, possible and positive. This is gained by modeling the behavior of an exemplar or by gathering relevant information from the environment. *(Like explaining the benefits of the new school to your child, he/she gaining new friends, and enjoying their new teacher.)*

Stage 3—Refreezing *(The idea that the change is good. It takes hold and change becomes real.)*
Integrate the new behaviors into the person's personality and attitudes. That is, stabilizing the changes requires testing to see if they fit—fit with the individual, and fit with the individual's social surroundings. Significant relationships are important people in the person's social environment—do these significant others accept and approve of the changes? (French, Bell, 82) *(The child embracing the new school and talk of the old school stopping.)*

Investments in Change

Front-end—Change Line from Point A to Point B—obstacles and paradigms are overcome at the beginning as illustrated by the slowly straightening arrows that represent the ***assimilation of change.***

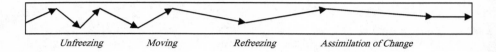

Unfreezing Moving Refreezing Assimilation of Change

Back-end Change Line from Point A to Point B—this change line illustrates that a change has been neglected at the front end and problems occurred at the tail end which lead to the ***extinction of change.***

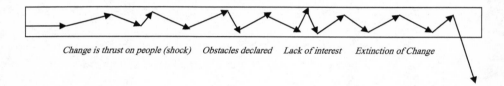

Change is thrust on people (shock) Obstacles declared Lack of interest Extinction of Change

Participation and Empowerment for Planned Change

Empowerment is not only relevant in our discussions about leadership but it is equally important to discuss empowerment when talking about change and innovation.

Refer to the Chapter on Motivation for a refresher on tips for empowerment. The excerpt below is a synopsis from research that links the importance of empowerment to involvement, participation, acceptance of decisions, increased commitment, lower stress levels, better solutions to problems and energized performance.

"One of the most important foundations of Organization Development (OD) is its use of participation/empowerment model. Participation in OD programs is not restricted to elites or the top people; it is extended broadly throughout the organization. Increased participation and empowerment have always been central goals and prominent values of the field. These pillars of OD practice

are validated by both research and practice. Research on group dynamics began in the 1940's and achieved exponential growth in the 1950s and 1960s. This research demonstrated that increased involvement and participation were desired by most people, had the ability to energize greater performance, produce better solutions to problems, and greatly enhanced acceptance of decisions. It was found that such group dynamics worked to overcome resistance to change, increased commitment to the organization, reduced stress levels, and generally made people feel better about themselves and their worlds. Participation is a powerful elixir—it is good for people, and it dramatically improves individual and organizational performance. To empower is to give someone power. This is done by giving individuals the authority to participate, to make decisions, to contribute their ideas, to exert influence, and to be responsible. This is why participation is such an effective form of empowerment. Participation enhances empowerment, and empowerment in turn enhances performance and individual well-being." (French, Bell, 94)

Creating a Participative, Empowered and Innovative Climate

Innovation is a more specialized kind of change, it is a new idea applied to initiating or improving a product, process or service, (Robbins, 571)

For innovation to occur, an environment of creativity, security, acceptance of failure, empowerment and adequate resources must be available. We will investigate throughout this chapter how to embrace innovation as a department and as an organization.

"Even crazy ideas may spark brilliance."

Have you ever been sitting around talking with friends, and someone says something ridiculous, but because of some little aspect of their ridiculous comment, your brain goes into a new direction, down the path to brilliance? Would your idea ever have come to fruition, if it weren't for the person coming out of left field in a seemingly unrelated way? It's hard to tell, but often what crazy, off-the-wall ideas do is cut through a lot of mundane thought that often gets mired in old paradigms.

Crazy ideas are often out of our comfort zone. Therefore, as we know, we have a tendency to negate or minimize ideas and people that aren't like us. The key to embracing and creating a climate that is participative, empowered and innovative is to be open-minded, encourage the absurd, weird and even ideas that seem nonsensical. It may just take you down the path to a solution. You never know from under which rock an idea may manifest.

"Diversity in thought creates innovative ideas."

Below are some ideas, strategies and guidelines to develop creative and innovative ideas to bridge gaps between what is desired and what is actually happening.

Brainstorming is a decision making technique in which group members present spontaneous, problem-solving suggestions to promote free, flexible, and creative thinking. It encourages group members to freely suggest alternatives, whether or not they will be used. No critical comments of any kind are allowed until all suggestions have been listed. In the sessions, members are encouraged to think aloud, and freewheeling is welcomed. The more novel and unusual the idea, the better. The object is to promote free, flexible thinking and to enable group members to build on one another's creativity. (Daft, Marcic, 196-197)

Brainstorming is recommended to go through a three stage process.

1. **Warm-up**—terms are defined for comprehension purposes.
2. **Freewheeling**—idea generation with documentation of each and every idea.
3. **Feasibility**—the whittling down of ideas that have promise.

One company in specific, IDEO, which is responsible for the development of over 3,000 product innovations or creations at the rate of 90 per year posts these rules for brainstorming in their workplace.

1. Defer Judgment
2. Build on the ideas of others
3. One conversation at a time
4. Stay focused on the topic and
5. Encourage wild ideas

Another effective and fun approach to idea generation is to choose one person to point out flaws in ideas, or in decisions. This person is the Devil's Advocate. The **Devil's Advocate** is a role set up to challenge the assumptions and assertions made by the group. The Devil's Advocate forces the group to rethink its approach to the problem and avoid reaching premature consensus or making unreasonable assumptions before proceeding with problem solutions.

Margaret Heffernan is an international business woman and author. She believes that disagreement is essential to breaking down barriers, and getting to the best solution. We must encourage disagreement? Margaret Heffernan believes we should.

Margaret Heffernan—*"Dare to Disagree"*
http://www.ted.com/talks/margaret_heffernan_dare_to_disagree.html

> *"When we dare to break silence or when we dare to see, when we create conflict we enable ourselves and those around us to do our very best thinking. Open information is fantastic, open networks are essential, but the truth won't set us free until we develop the skills, and the habits and the moral courage to use it. Openness isn't the end, it's the beginning."* (Margaret Heffernan)

The Devil's Advocate is a delicate position to be in because one is asking another person to rethink a position or opinion that most likely they have given much thought to. The benefit is that loopholes and pitfalls are easily exposed when a Devil's Advocate is placed in the mix. This person doesn't even have to be an expert in the subject area. Sometimes, it is even better if your Devil's Advocate is looking through innocent eyes. The obvious issues that no one can see because of familiarity can come to stark light.

Research Linking Innovation and Leadership

"Innovation and leadership are like Siamese twins,
they go everywhere together."

This excerpt is from a section on innovation from Kouzes and Posner's book, *The Leadership Challenge* and it explains the similarities and woven tapestry that is necessary for Leadership and Innovation to flourish. In fact, it appears that leadership is difficult without innovation and innovation is difficult without leadership.

*"In Mary Beth Kanter's research, a Harvard Business professor, she investigated the human resources practices and organization designs of innovation-producing organizations. She wanted to know what fostered and what hindered innovation in the US corporation. Our study and Kanter's were done quite independently of each other, at different periods of time, and with different purposes. We were studying leadership; Kanter was studying innovation. Yet when we compared Kanter's cases with ours, we were struck by their similarity. In some instances, Kanter's innovators and our leaders talked about nearly identical projects, yet they were in completely separate organizations in vastly different regions of the country. We and Kanter arrived at a similar conclusion in analyzing our respective cases: **leadership is inextricably connected with the process of innovation, of bringing new ideas, methods, or solutions into use**. To Kanter, innovation means change, and "change requires leadership . . . a prime mover' to push for implementation of strategic decisions."*

A "Prime Mover," as Kanter described—is you. It is your role as a leader to first understand that there is a gap or potential gap and then develop a plan to close it.

"Think of leadership without innovation and innovation without leadership as trying to start a fire without fuel, or oxygen.
They are each necessary for the
spark of creativity and innovation."

An innovative, empowered environment doesn't have to look different from any other environment; it is the results that are different. The processes are often very similar, it is the way the employees feel about the process—do they own it, believe it, and want it to succeed?

> *"What made you successful in the past, won't in the future."*
> (Lew Platt, Founder of Hewlett Packard)

> *"In today's fast changing world, decisions often must be made quickly, and an organization's ability to stimulate **the creativity and innovation skills of its employees is becoming increasingly important**. An environment in which bosses make all the decisions and hand them down to frontline workers is becoming not only inappropriate, but inefficient."* (Daft, Marcic, 196)

Advantages of Participative Decision Making for Change

As we've discussed in prior chapters, participation and empowerment can change the face of an organization, department or unit. To allow as many people into the fold as possible, to share knowledge, to share ideas, and gain support all while creating an atmosphere of collaboration and teamwork is powerful. Below are some advantages to fostering an innovative and creative workforce through participation and collaboration.

1. **Create a broader perspective** for defining the problem and diagnosing underlying causes and effects.
2. **More knowledge and facts** with which to identify potential solutions and produce more decision alternatives.
3. **More satisfaction with the decision** from the people who participate in the decision making process. They are more likely to support it.
4. **Increased support while facilitating implementation** will occur when participation is present.
5. **Reduces uncertainty for decision makers** who may be unwilling to undertake a big risk by themselves.

6. **Enhances member satisfaction** and produces support for a possibly risky situation. (Daft, Marcic, 195)

While there is power and commitment that comes from participative decision making, there are also some obstacles to consider and overcome. **Groupthink** is a phenomenon in which people are so committed to a cohesive in-group that their reluctance to express contrary opinions overrides their motivation to realistically consider alternatives. (Daft, Marcic, 196) If a group is like minded, discussion strengthens its prevailing opinions. For example, talking about racial issues increased prejudice in a high-prejudice group of high school students and decreased it in a low-prejudice group. (Myers, 565) Groupthink can occur from a lack of diversity, overconfidence from the leader, or unusually strong pressure to assimilate into a group.

Group think can be prevented by a leader who welcomes:

1. Various Opinions
2. Invite's Experts' Critique While Developing Plans
3. Assigns people to identify possible problems (Myers, 566.)

> *"As the suppression of dissent bends a group toward bad decisions, so open debate often shapes good decisions."*
> (David Myers)

Leading Change

Once a problem has been identified, and a solution has been foreseen, it is time to lead the change process. The change process can be looked at in two very different ways, proactive and reactive change. **Proactive change** is identifying a change initiative before it becomes a problem and creates a performance, need or process gap. Proactive change requires leaders to keep their fingers on the pulse of their area of responsibility. It lends itself to taking the time needed to ensure change can be nurtured and take root. It will also allow you to take the time to identify and remove barriers, or remove the weeds that will try to interfere with the health of your change. **Reactive change** is the enemy and is a response to an event that has already occurred.

The change has already taken place and reactive change is in response to a currently existing problem. Responses to reactive change can be "knee-jerk," and are often thrown at a problem to "stop the bleeding." We want our efforts in change to be proactive, not reactive.

We want our changes to address the root of the problem. This means finding the cause of the problem not symptoms of a greater problem. So often in business and healthcare we become aware of a problem, the symptoms of which are obvious but it takes time to understand the root problem. So instead, we pull the weed nut leave the root. Understanding comes through asking questions, taking our time, and then with understanding of the problem, taking action.

Unfortunately, as an example, we often come upon a problem, like a motorcycle accident, get out of our car and rush to the scene. We crouch down next to the cyclist. The cyclist has road rash all over him. We attend to the road rash and take great care of it, when really the problem lies in the blood pulsing from the cyclist's neck. When the paramedics arrive, we say, "Look how great we took care of the road rash." The paramedics respond with, "We can see that, but he bled out from his neck." We must identify the cause of the problem, not the symptoms. Addressing symptoms is merely identifying an effect of the problem. Our objective is to solve the problem not to hide it or ignore it.

The list below consists of the essential activities required for leading change.

1. **Establish a sense of urgency**—identify potential crisis and opportunities.
2. **Create a guiding coalition**—a group with enough power to lead the change. Change will not take hold, if a strong enough coalition is not in place.
3. **Develop a vision and strategy**—to direct the change strategy.
4. **Communicate the change vision**—use every possible channel and opportunity to talk up and reinforce the vision and required behaviors.
5. **Empowering broad-based action**—get rid of obstacles to success, including systems and structures that constrain rather than facilitate. Encourage risk taking and experimentation.

6. **Generate short-term wins**—don't wait for the ultimate grand realization of the vision. As small victories accumulate, you make the transition from isolated initiative to an integral part of the business.

7. **Consolidate gains and produce more change**—with the well-earned credibility of previous successes, keep changing things in ways that support the vision.

8. **Anchor new approaches in the culture**—highlight positive results, communicate the connections between the new behaviors and the improved results and keep developing new change agents and leaders. (Bateman, Snell, 587)

The ultimate goal is to establish a work environment where every person works toward something greater than themselves; something they can be proud of. It is about closing the gap between what someone needs and what someone is getting. The gap wasn't closed for the cyclist. Change is a good thing if we look at it through the right lens. It makes our work life easier, with more control, input and decision making capacity.

Innovation is scary because it's the unknown. We've certainly all been given the chance to offer an idea and, whammo, it goes viral. Everyone loves it. That environment could be a reality if we tap into the unfulfilled desires of employees and help them to Shine! like they all want to. Or we can crush ideas before they leave the tips of tongues and squelch the entire creative, spontaneous and innovative spark the group desperately needed.

To look out for each other's safety and well-being and to encourage the success of our co-workers is powerful medicine when teamwork and morale are ill. What better remedy could come than that from a workmate? You Shine!, and so do they. Absenteeism, turnover, staffing, worker's comp and unemployment ratings would all move in the right direction on the weekly spreadsheet that monitors you, and life would be good . . . (I know, click your heels Dorothy)

. . . . but, we've had these experiences before in our lives, so we know they are possible, why not try to make it happen, again. Think about how alive you felt, looking down from the clouds, wishing you could work more . . . . wait, no, no, no, no . . . it's about working smarter, doing it with a better attitude, and doing it for the right reasons. It's about involvement. Allowing people to actively participate in their work-life and feel good about it is the goal.

Maybe it was the feeling you got talking to a parent, best friend, coach or teacher. We all want to feel better about ourselves; we all need validation for our hard work and we all need to believe in someone else. Then, it bleeds into our families and our patients, and a cultural change has taken root.

> *"With each change, an opportunity for participation presents itself. Your job as the leader is to take that opportunity and give the team power. Ask their opinion and wade through the problems together so you all can be proud at the back-end when you solved the root problem."*

Chapter 6—Ethics and Recognition

A Brief History

"Ethical decisions breed ethical decisions, and of course, the converse is true, unethical decisions breed unethical decisions."

Ethical decision making has been mauled, squished, crushed, and put back together for millennia. Since the days of Plato who was a disciple of Socrates, and Aristotle, who was a student of Plato in and around the 3rd century B.C, the question of what is right, what is wrong and what is acceptable to a given culture with given norms has been at the forefront of the debate for thousands of years. Generally, "what ought I do?" is the question that is attempted to be answered. The issue is that people see the world differently and because of this, various approaches to ethics have been developed.

As time has unfolded and great thinkers have come and gone, a set of theories have fallen into place regarding the motivation and beliefs that allow a person to either make an ethical or unethical decision. Remember, **motivation** is an inner drive that directs a person's behavior toward goals. So then the question becomes what are the goals that motivate a person. In a workforce setting these goals can drive ethical decision making, or encourage unethical decision making. It is what the business culture values that influences the employee's decision. This is the link from ethics to recognition. If we recognize employees for work that is of an ethical nature, we will encourage an ethical culture to develop. If we emphasize and recognize profit over principle, we will foster an unethical environment. But first, what are ethics? **Ethics** are the code of moral principles and values that governs the behaviors of a person or group with respect to what is right or wrong. Ethics sets standards as to what is good or bad in conduct and decision making. (Robbins, 109)

The entire point of understanding what ethics are is to understand what causes unethical behavior and what to do when one encounters an ethical dilemma. This is the crux of the question over the years. An **ethical dilemma** arises in a situation when each alternative choice or behavior is undesirable because of potentially harmful ethical consequences. Right or wrong is not clearly defined. (Daft, Marcic, 109)

> *"If you sense an ethical inconsistency,*
> *trust your gut and seek guidance."*

A major consideration in making ethical decisions is whether or not our motivation is from a place of **intrinsic motivation** which calls people to action from an internal need to fulfill some outcome for personal satisfaction such as being all they can be, or helping another person for the sake of the deed. This would lend itself to an environment of ethical behavior. **Extrinsic motivation,** on the other hand, calls people to action from an external need to fulfill some outcome, such as money, power, prestige or notoriety and this can cause an unethical culture due to people acting from a suboptimum place in order to gain recognition or extrinsic rewards and often at the expense of another person, process or procedure.

So with this said, the link between ethical and unethical behavior is influenced by the culture an organization creates and what is valued and recognized by organizational leadership. We will look later at what encourages an unethical culture and what encourages an ethical culture.

Some of the ethical issues that have become prevalent in modern medicine are outlined below as well as the responsibility businesses have to maintain an ethical culture. Ethics permeate all work environments, but to examine two environments a

little more closely, we will look at medical ethics and general business ethics.

"During the past three or four decades, the concerns of medical ethics expanded dramatically. This has been due both to advances in medical technology and to the desire of a better informed public to participate in medical decision making. Technological advances have driven concern beyond the physician's dilemma of being both an indispensable healer-comforter, and thereby also a favored moneymaker, to the profound dilemmas associated with womb rentals, artificial insemination, genetic engineering, behavior control, organ transplantation, human experimentation, withholding or withdrawing treatment, neonatal euthanasia, and so forth. The list goes on and on.
In addition, the public—better informed, more alert to patient rights, and willing to pursue malpractice litigation—has fractured the mystique of the physician as the all-wise, not to be questioned, trusted custodian of life and death. Accordingly, moral problems associated with the doctor/patient relationship have risen. These moral problems include informed consent, confidentiality, paternalism, truth-telling, and so forth. Increasingly, colleges of medicine have responded to this expanding domain of medical ethics by infusing the traditional medical curriculum with courses in medical humanities." (Borchert, Stewart, 243.)

This phenomenon in medicine, as it is in business, is partly caused by the same forces that have caused the Changing Management Paradigm as we discussed in Chapter 1. With increased knowledge and education, and people desiring different things from life and work, the idea that we are equal can't help but flow into the arena of medicine and, for that matter, every other aspect of business.

"Governmental legislation, as well as public opinion, now requires companies to be good citizens and to be concerned for the general welfare of the community as a whole. The range of moral issues that affect a corporation's activities is vast, and is growing yearly in the public's view. These issues include the treatment of its employees, the company's role in assuring the safety and dependability of its products, its attitude toward the environment and restrictions placed upon

*it to prevent pollution of the air and waterways, truth in
advertising, personnel policies (including affirmative action
and nondiscrimination in hiring and firing decisions), plant
relocation and its effect on jobs, to mention the most prevalent
topics."* (Borchert, Stewart, 275, 276.)

The growing concern from society for the environment and the well-being of its customers is an on-going concern for modern business. This is referred to as **social responsibility** which, like ethics, is easy to understand: it is distinguishing right from wrong, and doing right. It means being a good corporate citizen. The formal definition is management's obligation to make choices and take actions that will contribute to the welfare and interests of society as well as the organization. (Robbins, 117)

"Culture is the creator of ethical behavior."

Social responsibility has a four tiered system of operation. The first and most important tier is economic responsibility and, as you'll notice; ethical responsibility comes in third, right above the voluntary, discretionary responsibilities. Of course, ethics are irrelevant without profit and the ability to keep the doors open, but would an ethical culture create a more profitable organization? Would allowing people to be ethical and encouraging it, make them feel that they are participating in more worthwhile work? Barry Schwartz, the Dorwin Cartwright Professor of Social Theory and Social Action at Swarthmore College who frequently publishes editorials in the *New York Times* and applies his research in psychology to current events, argues, "Yes," in his lecture called, "Our Loss of Wisdom."

Barry Schwartz, *"Our Loss of Wisdom"*
http://www.ted.com/talks/lang/en/barry_schwartz_on_our_loss_of_wisdom.html

Below are the generally agreed upon levels of Social Responsibility. Interestingly enough, Barry Schwartz and Barack Obama disagree with these levels. The question is how we collectively agree with Wall Street leering over our shoulders that the Social Responsibility Levels may need adjusted.

"We must ask, not just is it profitable, but is it right?"
(Barack Obama)

"The virtue we need above all others is practical wisdom, because it is what allows other virtues; honesty, kindness, courage and so on to be displayed at the right time and in the right way. I think people want to be allowed to be virtuous."
(Barry Schwartz)

Four Tiers of Social Responsibility

1. **Economic Responsibility**—which, simply stated is, to be profitable. Nothing else matters if the business isn't profitable. This seems to inherently dictate how decisions are made in that profit is the main concern. The problem is when profit is not adequately reinvested into the organization and its employees. This causes added strain on employees, customers and patients, at the profit of investors. So many economic goals are short-term which leads to a slow, not so gentle demise of the organization, in some cases.

2. **Legal Responsibility**—obey the law. If you obey the law because you want to and think it is right, and not because you have to, the chances of an ethical decision are greater.

3. **Ethical Responsibility**—be ethical, do what is right. Avoid harm. When profits, prestige, and power are encouraged over ethical behavior, which means people are tempted to side step ethics to gain power or position, the will of the organization, simply put, is to be profitable at any cost. This creates an untrusting, backstabbing environment where people often undermine their co-workers for their own benefit. This is a slippery slope and may work well for a few, but not the greater good.

4. **Discretionary Responsibility**—is voluntary and guided by a company's desire to make social contributions not mandated by economics, laws, or ethics. i.e.—charitable events.

As you can see ethics fall down the totem of importance. It is often difficult to maintain an ethical culture when the first question asked is, "Is this profitable?" and the second question asked is, "Is this legal?" Ethics often become an afterthought in the decision making process. The difference between legal and ethical is sometimes a fine line, but,

"Not always what is legal is ethical and vice versa."

Ethics and Legality

An act can be unethical but legal or an act can be illegal but ethical. It just depends on the situation and the ethical backbone of the person viewing the situation, not to mention the organization's position on ethics. Religious or non-religious views often determine whether a person views an act as ethical or not, even if the government says the activity is legal. For example, birth control, abortion and same sex marriage, but let's look at something a little less polarizing. We all speed, right? We all know that it is illegal to speed, and we all know that within 7-9 miles per hour over the speed limit we are probably safe. Safe? Safe from what? Getting a ticket, or injuring another person? Generally both, so ethically, we all agree that it is o.k. to speed within these limits. The probability of harm at that level of law breaking is ethically worth the risk. However ethical it is, it is still illegal. There are many viewpoints and paradigms' surrounding the idea of ethics and what makes one person ethical and another not. Below we will briefly look at a few of these perspectives.

Various Ethical Perspectives

"We are all changing, actualizing potentialities. Over some of these changes we have virtually no control, such as the sudden pain from a bee sting or the excretion of certain glands. Over other changes we exercise control, and we call these changes or motions voluntary. The task of ethics is to analyze and assess the nature of and conditions associated with these voluntary motions. In other words, ethics analyzes and assesses the potentialities that are open to human beings, and seeks

> *to provide guidance for humans when they are confronted by*
> *competing, alternative potentialities."* (Borchert, Stewart, 133)

With each of these various perspectives, a different approach is argued to explain the reasons people make decisions of an ethical or unethical nature, but of course that is still relative. Like leadership, motivation, communication and the various generations, everyone has different ideas, experiences, and reasons for their behavior. Ethics is no different. People see the world differently and the best and most productive way to understand why people do what they do is to learn the various reasons and thought processes behind the behavior.

Egoism is an ethical system that defines acceptable behavior as that which maximizes consequences for the individual. "Doing the right thing," the focus of moral philosophy, is defined by egoism as, "do the act that promotes the greatest good for oneself." If everyone follows this system, the well-being of society as a whole should increase. (Bateman, Snell, 143)

The issue with this perspective is that if everyone looks out for their own self-interest, there is no group or team, just individuals. This philosophy develops more readily in a capitalistic society but is unsustainable for the overall well-being of the whole. If it were practical then humans would never have joined in small bands of people and the exchange of ideas that sparked innovation and rapid technology advancement, would not have occurred. This philosophy seems counter intuitive to what we know about human behavior and development.

For example, imagine an egoist is propositioned with this ethical dilemma—an army is coming through town and it is going to wipe out everyone in its path, except you. Or, you can sacrifice yourself and save all one hundred thousand people from perishing. An egoist would say that they will let everyone else die, because their life is as important as or more important than everyone else's. The action works for them, regardless as to what happens to everyone else.

"I'll do what's right, right for me."

Utilitarianism is an ethical system that believes that decisions should be made with the greatest good in mind. It is nearly opposite of Egoism. This means that for a decision to be ethically sound, the greatest number of people would benefit from the decision even if a few had to suffer. Given the example of the army invading above, a Utilitarian would most likely sacrifice themselves for the greater good of the community with the idea that at least one person who was spared would have a greater impact on the well-being of the group and for certain all the people kept alive would have a greater positive effect than just one person left in place of the whole. This philosophy encourages groups to look out for one another. This system requires bravery, not martyrdom.

"I will sacrifice myself if I believe it is better for the entire group."

Relativism is based on the opinions and behaviors of other people within the person's sphere of influence. The relativist holds that there are only the norms that a particular society sets up, and these norms vary greatly from one society to another. (Borchert, Stewart, 68) A **norm** is a shared belief about how people should think and behave. (Bateman, Snell, 450.)

To a relativist the scenario we mentioned above may play out like this: The person in the ethical dilemma would consult other people or experts, regarding norms and expectations of the cultural group and make a decision based on input from others as to which course of action most aligns with the norms of the group. The best evidence to support this perspective is that different cultures around the world have very different ideas as to what is right and wrong. It is the environment, the people, the norms and expectations of a culture that dictate ethical lines of behavior.

"If the group thinks it is best and it is in-line with our norms, we'll take that action."

Determinism states that humans do not have free choice, that every event is precipitated by an event which makes a person act. There are no other possible alternatives to the decision making process. It has already been decided based on the cause driving one to act. A determinist in our scenario would react possibly like this, "What's meant to be will be. If I'm the one the army chooses to spare, then it wasn't my time to go. There's a plan for everyone." This unfortunately is a very passive and defeatist approach to decision making and life in general for that matter. If we have no control and everything is going to happen the way it is going to happen, then why care about it or anything else? For example, if something good was to happen to you, you would not be able to feel any sense of ownership to the event or pride in accomplishing something good. Likewise, on the contrary, if something bad happens, or you do something bad, it wasn't your fault, it was already determined to be.

"It doesn't matter. It's out of my control."

Moral Rights perspective believes that human beings should not have fundamental rights infringed upon or taken away due to an ethical decision. If those rights are abridged the moral rights advocate believes the decision is unethical. Thus, an ethically correct decision is one that best maintains the rights of those people affected by it. (Daft, Marcic, 112)

Some of the moral rights that are considered during the decision making process are;

1. **The right of free consent**—Individuals are to be treated only as they knowingly and freely consent to be treated.
2. **The right to privacy**—individuals can choose to do as they please away from work and have control of information about their private lives.
3. **The right to freedom of conscience**—individuals may refrain from carrying out any order that violates their moral or religious norms.
4. **The right to free speech**—individuals may criticize truthfully the ethics or legality of actions of others.
5. **The right to due process**—individuals have a right to an impartial hearing and fair treatment.
6. **The right to life and safety**—individuals have a right to live without endangerment or violation of their health and safety.

This is the most applicable approach to developing an ethical culture within a work group or organization. It provides guideposts for decision making and takes into account the very nature of ethical decision making. It provides rights to those who are affected by the decisions and gives the decision maker's checkpoints to ensure a violation in ethics does not occur.

"It is every human beings right to be treated ethically."

Justice approach states that moral decisions must be based on standards of equity, fairness, and impartiality. (Daft, Marcic, 112) This approach coupled with the moral rights approach is a strong ally in the development of an ethically sound workforce. It is also the most closely aligned with that of a learning organization and the principles and fundamentals we have discussed thus far. To look deeper into the justice approach, there are three types of justice, leaders should be concerned with:

1. **Distributive justice**—requires that different treatment of people must not be based on arbitrary reasons. Individuals who are similar in respects relevant to a decision should be treated similarly.
2. **Procedural Justice**—means that rules must be administered fairly. They should be stated concisely and clearly and should be impartially enforced.
3. **Compensatory Justice**—argues that individuals should be compensated for the cost of their injuries by the party responsible. (Daft, Marcic, 113)

"It is the leader's role to determine the ethical guideposts of their unit, above and beyond the organization's standards."

"Managers bring specific personality and behavioral traits to the job. Personal needs, family influence, and religious background all shape a manager's value system." (Daft, Marcic, 114)

Not only are the Moral Rights and Justice Approaches consistent with business norms, they are consistent with business law and our world of work. They both squarely give the leader and the people involved a basis for developing, controlling and changing the ethical cultures within their unit or organization. For a leader to influence the ethical underpinnings of an organization or unit, it is important to understand the ethical development people progress through. This way you will be able to determine which level of ethical development you will be dealing with, given a certain individual or group, and even assess where you are as a leader.

Personal Moral Development

The diagram and passage below is based on Lawrence Kohlberg's work and it has been taken from the Third Edition of *Understanding Management* by Richard Daft, and Dorothy Marcic. Kohlberg divided the Personal Moral Development of human beings into three distinct levels.

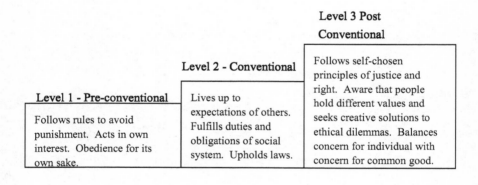

Level 3 Post Conventional

Follows self-chosen principles of justice and right. Aware that people hold different values and seeks creative solutions to ethical dilemmas. Balances concern for individual with concern for common good.

Level 2 - Conventional

Lives up to expectations of others. Fulfills duties and obligations of social system. Upholds laws.

Level 1 - Pre-conventional

Follows rules to avoid punishment. Acts in own interest. Obedience for its own sake.

Level 1 or Pre-Conventional Stage—(Extrinsically Motivated) of moral development finds people concerned with external rewards and punishments, and they obey authority to avoid detrimental personal consequences. In an organizational context, this level may be associated with managers who use an autocratic or coercive leadership style, with employees oriented toward dependable accomplishment of specific tasks. This is the behavior of a child, "Will I get in trouble or not?" It isn't about right or wrong, it's about consequences.

Level 2 or Conventional Stage—(Extrinsically Motivated) people learn to conform to the expectations of good behavior as defined by colleagues, family, friends, and society. Meeting social and interpersonal obligations is important. Work group collaboration is the preferred manner for accomplishment of organizational goals, and managers use a leadership style that encourages interpersonal relationships and cooperation. Most people stay at this level of ethics.

Level 3 or Post-Conventional Stage—(Intrinsically Motivated) of moral development finds that individuals are guided by an internal set of values and standards and will even disobey rules or laws that violate these principles. Internal values become more important than the expectations of significant others. As an example, when the USS *Indianapolis* sank after being torpedoed during WWII, one Navy pilot disobeyed orders and risked his life to save men who were being picked off by sharks. The pilot was operating from the highest level of moral development in attempting the rescue despite a direct order from superiors. Life and experience, religion and philosophy dictate how this person will react to ethical situations. These decisions will be well thought out and in-line with the person making the decision's ethical guideposts above and beyond what the organization's ethical guideposts are.

When leaders operate from the highest level of development, they use transformative or servant leadership (as discussed in Chapter 3, The Differences Between Leadership and Management) focusing on the needs of followers and encouraging others to think for themselves and to engage in higher levels of moral reasoning. Employees are empowered and given opportunities for constructive participation in governance of the organization. The great majority of managers operate at level two. A few have not advanced beyond level one. Only about 20% of American adults reach the level three stage of moral development. People at level three are able to act in an independent, ethical manner regardless of expectations from others inside or outside the organization. Managers at level three of moral development will make ethical decisions whatever the organizational consequences for them. (Daft, Marcic, 114-115)

Guidelines for Ethical Decision Making

When we are deliberating about whether or not to make a decision because of moral or ethical issues, we often ask ourselves how a significant person in our life may respond to the decision, or we may even ask ourselves if we will be able to sleep at night. These are our own internal guideposts for decision making. I'm sure many of us have said to ourselves,

"I'm the one who has to live with myself."

Of course this means you want the decision to be a good one; one you can be proud of and feel good talking to others about. In addition to the personal guideposts we all have, the guidelines below for ethical decision making will whittle down the concerns one may have before they get to the other side of a tough ethical decision. These will not tell us exactly what to do or how to do it, but they will help bring to light some tough considerations during the process of making an ethical decision.

1. **Don't make assumptions**—Is the problem/dilemma really what it appears to be? If you are not sure, find out.
2. **Is it legal/ethical**—if you are not sure the action you are taking is legal and/or ethical, find out.
3. **How will you feel**—if you take an action?
4. **Is it reasonable**—do you understand the position of those who oppose the action you are considering? Remember, you can't argue a point until you know the other person's point of view.
5. **What are the effects**—who does the action benefit, harm, and for how long and how much.
6. **Transferability**—Would you be willing to allow everyone to do what you are considering doing?
7. **Consult experts**—Have you sought the opinion of others who are knowledgeable on the subject and who would be objective?
8. **Are you proud of the decision**—would your action be embarrassing to you if it were made known to your family, friends, co-workers or superiors?

Danger Signs of an Unethical Culture

People often give in to what they perceive to be pressures or preferences of powerful others. States Professor Arthur Brief of Tulane University, "If the boss says, 'Achieve a specific sales or profit target, period.' I think, people will do their very best to achieve those directions even if it means sacrificing their own values. They may not like it, but they define it as part of the job." (Bateman, Snell, 148)

With this, it is very clear that ethical behavior starts at the top and is pushed down. The key is that everyone in the organization, especially the executive leaders, are pushing a culture down that is ethical, socially responsible and in-line with the expectations of the environment.

In organizations, it is an on-going challenge to maintain consistent ethical behavior by all employees. What are some danger signs that an organization may be allowing or even encouraging unethical behavior among its people? Many factors create a climate conducive to unethical behavior, including:

1. Excessive emphasis on short term revenues over longer-term considerations.
2. Failure to establish a written code of ethics.
3. A desire for simple, "quick fix" solutions to ethical problems.
4. An unwillingness to take an ethical stand that may impose financial costs.
5. Consideration of ethics solely as a legal issue or a public relations tool.
6. Lack of clear procedures for handling ethical problems.
7. Response to the demands of shareholders at the expense of other considerations. (Bateman, Snell, 148)

Using Recognition and Positive Reinforcement to Develop an Ethical Culture

After digging into the nature of ethical decision making, the fundamentals of how people make ethical decisions and how human moral development occurs, it is apparent that we as leaders have a considerable amount of control regarding the environment we create in our worlds of work.

We discussed reinforcement in the section on Motivation. There were four types of reinforcement used to change a person's behavior; punishment, extinction, avoidance learning and positive reinforcement. The first three are more or less negative approaches to changing a person's behavior. What we are going to focus on is the positive reinforcement or recognition for desired behavior. **Positive Reinforcement** is to actively give pleasant and positive feedback for a desired behavior whether verbal, or another form.

If for example, an organization recognizes or rewards employees for getting the job done below budget, the likelihood of employees working to keep the project under budget will become paramount because that is what the emphasis is on. With a focus like this, employees may be more inclined to cut corners, use suboptimum supplies, and inevitably, quality will suffer.

On the other hand, if an organization such as a hospital rewards or recognizes employees for compliments, positive patient comments, teamwork, collaboration, improved patient satisfaction scores or quality outcomes, the likelihood of employees focusing their attention on these items is greater which, in turn, should positively affect the bottom line. We often take an upside down approach which is to say we focus on making money at any cost and then focus on doing it right. This approach creates a lot of work at the back-end, once the culture has been created, to regain the confidence of employees, patients and customers.

> *"As the leader, be the culture you want to create—*
> *live it, practice it and tell people about it."*

Recognition for a job well done is not only a great motivator to continue to perform at high levels, but it is a terrific source of self-esteem. Remember, for an employee to reach self-actualization, they need to have high self-esteem according to Maslow. Often leaders feel like their employees are "just doing what they are paid to do." That is the truth but, as a leader, if you want to encourage continued affirmative behavior, recognition will provide the vehicle for higher satisfaction, and improved performance. In one study done by Dr. Bob Nelson, President of Nelson Motivation Inc.,

> *"Workers were asked to rank a list of motivators from 1-10 in order of importance. Workers rated 'appreciation for a job well done,' as the #1 motivator; supervisors ranked it #8. Employees ranked 'feeling in on things,' as the #2 in importance; their managers ranked it #10."* (Nelson)

Again, this is a very good illustration of the gaps that sometimes exist between leaders and employees. One of our jobs as leaders is to close gaps. If employees want recognition for a job well done and want to feel, "in on things," which means communication and empowerment, then we as leaders must give them what they need for them to Shine! While at the same time, we as leaders will create an environment conducive to teamwork, accountability, improved morale and lower turnover.

Keys to Positive and Effective Recognition

It is advisable for each unit leader to develop attainable and measurable goals. These goals should reflect the larger organization's goals and the two should feed each other with energy. The guidelines below will help you ensure your efforts in recognition toward ethical behavior are not wasted.

1. **Instantaneous Recognition**—reward the behavior when it happens, timing is very important, don't delay praise. DON'T WAIT . . . TAKE THE TIME! Example; "I see you are in a meeting with Pat . . . however I wanted to let you know the way you responded to Dr. Smith today was very impressive! When you are done here can we talk in my office?"
2. **Be Sincere**—Words seem hollow if you are not sincere in why you're praising. Eye contact . . . body language . . . STOP . . . don't keep walking . . . take the time! TONE OF VOICE. So often leaders say things in passing or with their hand on the door. This sends a poor message. Ask them to come to

your office or go to them specifically to tell them good job. Especially do this if the only time they usually see you is because of criticism.

3. **Be Specific**—Avoid generalizations in favor of details of the achievement or action. This gives the act of praise more meaning. It gives the recognizable deed more relevance. Again be specific . . . "Lisa I was glad I was in the department this morning to hear how you explained Mrs. Jones' imaging procedure to her. You were able to put her at ease and obviously made her feel better about the process."

4. **Personal Praise**—When possible, convey your praise in person, face to face. Technology is a wonderful thing . . . however . . . not in this instance.

5. **Be Positive and Stay Positive**—do not undercut praise with a concluding note of criticism. Take the opportunity of the situation and make it a positive. Do not do this . . . "Marge you did an excellent job handling Mr. Johnson's issues. Those anti-depressants must really be working."

6. **Be Proactive**—Praise progress toward goals, otherwise you'll tend to react to the negative—typically mistakes—in your interactions with others.

"No one ever gets tired of hearing thank you."

Creating Positive Feedback

When you give someone feedback, or praise, it is important that the person walks away feeling good about it. The worst case scenario is that the employee walks away feeling patronized or pacified. To ensure your attempts at recognition are valuable, try following these basic guidelines as described by Dr. Bob Nelson.

1. **I saw what you did**—the employee doesn't know what you see, but if you explain to them exactly why what they did was so powerful, they will be encouraged to continue that behavior. It is an opportunity to use clear, concise language to have a very positive conversation. For example,

*"I saw you walking down the hall and as you passed each bed,
you stopped in to see if anyone needed anything."*

2. **I appreciate what you did**—place value on the behavior or achievement. Explain how what the employee did pushes the employee and unit closer to meeting the agreed upon goals. For example,

    "I appreciate you doing that because it demonstrates teamwork, and that you are concerned with the patients, even if they aren't yours."

3. **Explain why it is important**—provide context to the situation, and illustrate how the action may have affected others on the periphery of the situation or how it was important to operations, goals, or the unit. For example,

    "This is important because it demonstrates to others that we are all in this together, and it illustrates to staff that you are truly here for the patient. You set a good example."

4. **Here's how it made me feel**—give an emotional charge. Explain how what they did made you feel or how it made another person feel.

    "I was proud of you and you made me feel very good about having you in our unit. I know you'll keep the best interests of patients in mind. You're a good nurse."

Ideas for Recognition and Involvement Programs

A few years back, 1,500 employees were surveyed in a variety of work settings to find out what they considered to be the most powerful workplace motivator. Their response? Recognition, recognition, recognition! (Robbins, 192)

Employee recognition programs can consist of giving approval, personal attention, expressing interest and, of course, appreciation for excellent work. At the BIC Corporation in Milford, Connecticut, which makes pens, razors and cigarette lighters, production employees meet every week to review offerings from the employee suggestion box. Whenever a group voices its support for a proposal, it is immediately passed on to the appropriate supervisor, who has 10 days to put the change in place. (Robbins, 193)

Active Leadership

Being an active, engaged leader is the most important aspect of leading the recognition initiative. You must be visible, approachable and open to suggestions with a non-biased attitude. Employees must feel as if you are their ally in process improvement, teamwork, participation and communication. The employee must feel no hesitation when they have an idea or concern to share with you.

Tips for Presenting Yourself as an Active Leader

1. **Walk around**—get to know each employee personally.
2. **Emphasize the positive**—focus your attention on what employees do well.
3. **Use negatives as an opportunity**—when something goes wrong, use it as an opportunity to teach the employee, not scold. This will make employees more open to be creative and find solutions if they know you will be a resource for them.
4. **Listen**—when an employee approaches you, listen to them fully. Do not rebut, or interrupt—let them get to their point. Refer to Chapter Two on Communication, for ideas.

Suggestion Box

In no way will the following be as effective as the prior suggestion, but they are a good supplement to solid, active leadership. This gives employees a say in their work. It is recommended that even if the larger organization has a suggestion box, a unit specific suggestion box still be used. It also sets the stage for people to avoid complaining unless they are willing to make a suggestion for improvement. Some ideas for implementing a unit specific suggestion box are:

1. **Discuss suggestions as a group**—let the group weigh in on the validity of the idea and let the group figure out how it will work, or won't work.
2. **Implement suggestions as a team**—once an idea has been accepted, discuss as a group who will do what and how. Let assignments be divided out by the group.
3. **Recognize the author**—when a suggestion is used, recognize the idea generator publicly.

Recognition Board

This provides a place for employees, patients, customers, and other co-workers to see how well others are doing. It may also inspire others to change their behavior so they can find themselves on the recognition board. Again, even if the organization as a whole has a recognition board, try setting up a unit specific board. Be sure to consider these factors as you move forward.

1. **Public**—recognize employees so others can see how great they are.
2. **Different People**—ensure different people are responsible for updating the board and changing the format of the board, maybe with seasonal themes, etc. This will create a sense of community, that everyone is responsible and encourage more pride in the effort.
3. **Recognize the Small Things**—as well as the big things. Recognition for both small and large deeds encourages others to follow suit and behave in ways that are favorable to the goals of the department which ultimately should provide satisfaction to employees because they helped develop the goals.

Tokens of Appreciation

A token of appreciation could be a thank you note. It is wise to standardize these notes. It isn't uncommon for people to hang them in their workspace to show them off. If everyone knows what they are, they gain more interest and attention. Refer to Creating

Positive Feedback and Keys to Positive and Effective Recognition in this section to ensure you don't leave any opportunity unstoked. The tokens of appreciation could also be stickers, or even small monetary awards, gift certificates and the like.

The advantage to implementing these strategies is that people will begin to self-monitor themselves. They will know what is expected, what they need to do to thrive and how they need to do it. Remember, the more employees that can work independently and handle their business with critical thinking skills and make the right decision within the policy and procedural guidelines of the organization, the more time you as the leader will have to focus on bringing people up to their maximum potential and do what every leader is charged with doing—making people better.

Developing an Ethical Culture through Goals and Recognition

No matter what the organizational goals are, the unit goals should enhance and perpetuate the attainment of the overall organizational goals. The unit goals should also be attainable and easily measured. Employees should be able to monitor the attainment of goals and have direct impact on reaching the departmental goal which will feed the organizational goals.

To ensure that these goals are agreeable to employees, attainable, specific and measurable develop these goals as a group. This process will give the employees power to affect their own work-life. Empowerment is a critical aspect in the attainment of goals. Employees need to feel like they have control over the success or failure of goal attainment. If a leader and team develop mutually acceptable goals, the likelihood that employees will buy-in, commit and make it happen is greater. There shouldn't be too many goals at once because people can get bogged down and lose focus especially if they are being pulled in different directions.

"Fix one problem at a time and do it well.
Don't attempt multiple priorities at once and expect anything
but mediocre results."

Once a goal has been attained, celebrate and recognize those that contributed to the success. Each time you as the leader see an employee working toward the goal, acknowledge them and tell them, "good job." This will encourage them to continue the behavior, and it helps their self-esteem. It will eliminate ambiguity and allow people to feel good about their work, knowing that what they are doing is bigger than them. It will remind them that they do have important and meaningful jobs.

Remember, the goals should be in-line ethically with the organization, your department and what you are trying to accomplish. The goals should be measurable issues that will create a culture of ethical behavior not tempt people to be unethical. For example, focus on small things like lessening the response time to call bells, or decreasing defects by 2%. Monitor it, track it and encourage people to respond quickly. **"Answer the Why,"** and explain to them that the quicker we respond to call bells the more pleasant the patients will be and the more pleasant the employee's work day will be. Remember, the investment at the front-end of an experience will make the back-end run smoother. When they do respond quickly to call bells, let them know and tell them good job and that you appreciate it. Goals like this will encourage a culture of care, and motivation for the right reasons. They may even get to go home to their families with good attitudes which then can turn into a cycle of positivity which bleeds back into their work-life.

Chapter 7—Employment Law and Interviewing Effectively—(Hire Hard so you can Manage Easy)

A Brief Introduction

One could argue that this section should be covered first in any leadership discussion, because having the right people from the onset is much easier than training, or developing the wrong person to be right, after the fact. The fundamental aspect to developing and creating a lasting team of people who will work together for the right reasons and strive for positive results is **Staffing,** which is the mutual process by which the individual and the organization become matched to form the employment relationship. (Heneman, Heneman, Judge, 4)

However, most leaders do not have the luxury of hiring their staff from the inception of their department. Most leaders are not in a start-up mode; they are scrambling and trying to fill vacancies for staffing fluidity. **Staffing fluidity** is to minimize turnover, and maximize retention. This in turn cuts down on orientation costs, downtime from staff, inconsistency in care, and provides a more secure and functional work unit. It is no different than a sports team trying to put a new player into the lineup each week. The new player is more likely to run the wrong play simply due to inexperience with the team and unfamiliarity with the playbook. The great teams that find tremendous success have stable members that know each other's work patterns, and habits. They know what to expect and uncertainty and ambiguity are diminished.

Just like in the process of Change Management, we want to invest our effort at the front—end of the employment relationship so that the change or new employee takes hold, prospers and grows. We want to **Hire Hard so we can Manage Easy** which simply put is to invest our effort and energy during the interview process so that we make good, long lasting hiring decisions to avoid doing it again three months later, or manage and discipline a person with a bad attitude, poor work performance or skills. The worst place for a department or team to be in is that members are coming and going all the time. This creates uncertainty and unfamiliarity and inhibits growth by the team members who are left behind, training the new people with limited resources due to turnover.

> *"Invest time, energy and thoughtfulness into the front-end of the hiring process for long-term dividends in the form of fluidity, teamwork and consistency."*

Think of the hiring process as an opportunity to invest in your department's future, the continuity of the team, and the organization. It is not unlike a retirement investment. You want to make the right decision at the front-end and invest in a stock or employee that has a proven track record that fits your needs and will provide a long-term dividend in the form of continued growth, employment and a return on your investment at the back-end.

To mirror the hiring process as an investment, we want to find the right person that will fit your department's needs, while at the same time the department and team will fit the candidate's needs and provide long-term stability to each. The relationship has to be mutually beneficial or it will not work.

A side effect of proper hiring and finding the correct fit is that the leader has more time to focus on the higher order needs of the department. If we compare staffing to **Maslow's Needs Hierarchy of Motivation**, staffing is like providing the basic needs for employees such as food, water, shelter and safety. Employees who are in a department that is constantly turning over and hiring new employees can't even reach the 3rd level or (social level) in the needs hierarchy due to constantly seeing new people and never really ever being able to get acquainted with them. It's very difficult to fulfill social, self-esteem and self-actualization needs when the daily work-life is tumultuous, unsteady and uncertain.

*"The ultimate goal of staffing is to provide stability so
that leaders and employees can focus on higher order need
fulfillment, such as quality improvement, patient satisfaction
and ultimately their own self-esteem and self-actualization."*

Federal Anti-Discrimination Laws

First and foremost in the hiring process, we want to do it legally and ensure everyone who applies is considered for employment without bias. Over the years, and because of employer abuse to employees, the federal government has put into place hundreds and maybe thousands of pieces of legislation for the protection of employees. The main trend with all of these laws is to prevent discrimination due to prejudice. To clarify the difference between prejudice and discrimination, **Prejudice** is a preconceived judgment or opinion, an adverse opinion or leaning formed without just grounds or before sufficient knowledge. (Websters) This is first and foremost what employment law is trying to avoid in the interview and hiring process. Prejudice can lead to discrimination which is ultimately what causes employment laws to be broken. To **Discriminate** is to make a difference in the treatment or favor on a basis other than individual merit, i.e, in favor of friends, or against a certain nationality. (Websters)

*"Prejudice is an irrational idea that passes judgment
unsubstantiated, and discrimination is acting on that prejudice."*

Employment laws are intended to prevent discrimination. However, only the mind of each individual decision maker can decide that they will not assign characteristics to a group without fully understanding the individual. Discrimination doesn't occur without prejudice and only the individual can decide whether they will or will not view a certain group, person or process without prejudice. Below are various employment laws that attempt to prevent discrimination and regardless of your personal experiences, you must obey them.

A. **Equal Employment Opportunity (EEO)**—refers to the treatment of individuals in all aspects of employment; hiring, promotion, training, termination, etc, in a fair and nonbiased manner. Every employer is bound by the EEO. This is a general statement that reflects the intent to remain unbiased in the employment relationship.

"Hire for knowledge, skills and abilities,
not other non-job related factors."

B. **Fair Labor Standards Act, 1938**—provides for a minimum wage and a maximum work week in which time over this maximum of 40 hours has to be paid at time and half. This act prohibits children from working before the age of 14 unless it is farm work. Children ages 14-15 cannot work in a hazardous occupation and cannot work more than 3 hours during a school day and 8 hours on a non-school day.

C. **The Equal Pay Act of 1963**—Requires all employees covered by the Fair Labor Standards Act and others to provide equal pay for equal work, regardless of sex.

"Equal pay for equal work—
performance is the differentiator, not gender."

D. **Title VII of the Civil Rights Act of 1964 and 1991**—Prohibits the discrimination of employment on the basis of race, color, religion, sex and national origin. Title VII of the Civil Rights Act of 1964 created the Equal Employment Opportunity Commission (EEOC) to enforce this act. The EEOC is the governing body that investigates and passes judgment on claims of discrimination. The Civil Rights Act of 1991 provides compensatory, punitive damages and jury trials in cases involving intentional discrimination and requires employers to demonstrate that job practices are job-related and consistent with business necessities. **Business Necessity** is a work related practice that is necessary to the safe and efficient operation of an organization. A **Bona Fide**

Occupational Qualification (BFOQ) is the exception and it is a characteristic providing a legitimate reason why an employer can exclude persons from otherwise illegal basis of consideration. (Mathis, Jackson, 77) For example, a male actor cannot file a claim of discrimination, if the role they auditioned for was for a female. Every claim is investigated.

E. **The Equal Employment Opportunity Act of 1972**—Amended Title VII of the Civil Rights Act of 1964 and strengthened the EEOC's enforcement powers and extends coverage of Title VII to government employees, employees in higher education, and other employers and employees.

F. **Pregnancy Discrimination Act of 1978**—Broadens the definition of sex discrimination to include pregnancy, childbirth, or related medical conditions. It prohibits employers from discriminating against pregnant women in employment benefits, or hiring decisions if they are capable of performing their job duties.

"Pregnancy is not a limitation on employment and is not a factor in employment decisions."

G. **Age Discrimination in Employment Act of 1967 (ADEA)**—was initiated to protect workers over 40 years of age against discrimination based on age in the areas of hiring, retention, promotion, compensation, and other areas of employment for companies with over 20 employees. It makes it illegal to require retirement to save on pension funding, to replace them with younger workers to save on wages, or pass over them for promotions. This act applies to any employer subject to Title VII. It also bans mandatory retirement before the age of 70.

"Age is not a limitation, or predictor of a candidate's performance."

H. Americans with Disabilities Act of 1990 (ADA)—This act extends coverage of the civil rights act of 1964. Employers cannot discriminate against any applicant with a disability that substantially limits this person's mental or physical ability. Of course this person has to be able to perform the essential functions of the job. Employers must provide **reasonable accommodation** (which is an attempt to adjust the working conditions or schedule for employees with disabilities) for any person who states they have a disability and can prove this disability and as long as the accommodation doesn't provide an **undue hardship** on the company. I.e. installing an elevator for a person without legs is not a reasonable accommodation, but moving an office to the first floor is. A disabled person is "any person who:

1. Has a physical or mental impairment which substantially limits one or more of such person's **major life activities**—walking, talking, seeing, hearing, etc 2. Has a record of such impairment, or 3. Is regarded as having such an impairment."

Interview Questions - Do's and Don'ts

Category	Non-Discriminatory Questions	Discriminatory Questions	Reasoning
National Origin	What is your name? Do you speak any foreign languages that may help?	Is that name Irish?	It doesn't matter where they are from. Violates Title VII.
Age	Are you over 18? What is your date of birth?	How old are you? the candidate is under 18.	Age is only a consideration if Violates ADEA. FLSA has different requirements for children under 18.
Gender	Don't say anything unless it is a BFOQ.	Do you go by Mr. of Ms.?	Gender doesn't matter. Could violate Equal Pay Act, EEO act, Pregnancy Discrimination Act.
Race	Don't say anything.	What is your race?	Race doesn't matter. Violates Title VII, EEO Act.
Disabilities	Are you disabled in any way that may affect job performance?	Do you have any physical defects?	Reasonable accommodations are to be made if possible. Violates ADA.
Height and Weight	Inappropriate unless it is a BFOQ.	How tall are you? How much do you weigh?	Doesn't matter. You can not base a hiring decision on height and weight.
Residence	What is your address? How long have you lived there?	Who do you live with? What are the names of the people you live with?	Hiring decisions cannot be based on marital status or if the candidate has children.
Religion	An employee needs to know what the required work schedule is.	Are you religious? What is your faith?	Some religions do not allow work on certain days. Religion is not a factor, but availability is.
Military Record	Have you had military experience or training related to position?	Were you honorably discharged?	Cannot ask what type of discharge was received. May indicate a disability.
Education and Experience	Where did you attend school? What experience do you have? Why did you leave prior employment? What was your salary?	Is that school affiliated with any religion? When did you graduate? What are your hobbies?	Religion is not related May indicate age and violates ADEA. Hobbies are irrelevant.
Criminal Record	Have you been convicted of a crime?	Have you been arrested?	There is a big difference between a conviction and an arrest.
Citizenship	Are you legally able to work in the United States?	Are you a U.S. citizen?	Being a U.S. citizen is not relevant because visas can be issued that allow non-citizens to work in the U.S.
Marital/Family Status	Who can we contact in case of an emergency	Are you married, divorced, single? Do you prefer Miss, Ms. or Mrs.? Do you have any children?	Employment decisions can not be based on these issues.

Interviewing Hard so you can Manage Easy

To accomplish our ultimate goal with staffing, which is to hire qualified people who are a good fit into the department and organization, we want to ensure we uncover all the stumbling blocks to employment before we make the job offer. It is so much easier to make a good investment at the front-end and watch it grow and pay back dividends in fluidity, teamwork and consistency. The strategies below will help guide us through this process so that we can make good, long lasting and mutually beneficial employment decisions.

10 Interviewing Strategies

The proper way to go into an interview is to make no assumptions and let the facts persuade you. The intangibles such as non-verbal cues, enthusiasm or lack of enthusiasm should be deciding factors between candidates that share an equivalent skill set. Remember, after minimum qualifications, fit is the key.

The following list presents ten guidelines for employment interviews that are commonly accepted and supported by research findings. Their apparent simplicity should not lead one to underestimate their importance.

1. **Establish an interview plan**—Examine the purposes of the interview and determine the areas and specific questions to be covered. Review job requirements, application-form data, and other available information before seeing the applicant. Look for questionable information in the application and resume and seek to gain understanding and clarification.

2. **Establish and maintain rapport**—This is accomplished by greeting the applicant pleasantly, by explaining the purpose of the interview, by displaying sincere interest in the applicant, and by listening carefully.

> *"The more comfortable a candidate is during an interview, the more likely they will show you their true selves."*

3. **Be an active listener**—Strive to understand, comprehend, and gain insight into what maybe suggested or implied. A good listener's mind is alert, and their face and posture reflect this fact. Refer to Chapter 2 on *Effective Communication*.

*"The interview isn't about you. It's about the candidate,
so stop talking and listen to them."*

4. Pay attention to nonverbal cues—An applicant's facial expressions, gestures, body position, and movements often provide clues to that person's attitudes and feelings. Interviewers should be aware of what they themselves are communicating nonverbally as well. We need to trust what those non-verbal cues tell us. I.e. body language, space language, paralanguage, and of course time language. If they are late, or do not have a sense of urgency—this can be a predictor of a future problem.

*"Non-verbal cues are the most ancient
form of human communication, trust your gut."*

5. Provide information as freely and honestly as possible—Answer fully and frankly the applicant's questions. Give the candidate a **Realistic Job Preview**, which details both the negatives and positives of the position. The point in giving the candidate the pros and cons of the job are so they can make an informed decision and hopefully a decision that will last. It doesn't make sense to the leader, candidate or potential co-workers to mislead or withhold information from a candidate. If they find out the job isn't what you told them, they will feel resentment, betrayal, and certainly a loss of confidence and trust in you as their leader. On the other hand, if you as their leader, "shoot straight," and tell them the full scope of the position, they will gain trust and confidence in your word and there will be no discrepancies in expectations. Besides, you don't want to trick someone into accepting a job, make them miserable and then find yourself doing the same "song and dance" to replace this person in a month or more.

"Tell the candidate the good, the bad and the ugly."

6. Use Questions—To elicit a truthful answer, questions should be phrased as objectively as possible, giving no indication of what response is desired. You don't want to "lead the witness," or suggest by the way you ask the question what the correct or desired response is. You want honest responses that will weed out candidates that may not be a good fit.

"Don't lead the candidate to the answer you want to hear."

7. Separate facts from inferences—During the interview, record factual information. Later, record your inferences or interpretations of the facts. Compare your inferences with those of other interviewers. Do not make assumptions. If you need clarification or there is inconsistency, just ask the person more questions to gain clarity. This is often where the real information is shared—through a follow-up question.

"We all know about assumptions."

8. Recognize biases and stereotypes—One typical bias is for interviewers to consider strangers who have interests, experiences, and backgrounds similar to their own to be more acceptable. Stereotyping involves forming generalized opinions of how people of a given gender, race, or ethnic background appear, think, feel and act. The influence of sex-role stereotyping is central to sex discrimination in employment. Avoid the influence of "beautyism." Discrimination against unattractive people is a persistent and pervasive form of employment discrimination. Also avoid the "halo effect" or judging an individual favorably or unfavorably overall on the basis of only one strong point (or weak point—horn effect) on which you place high value.

"Diversity is the spark of innovation."

9. Control the course of the interview—Establish an interview plan and stick to it. Provide the applicant with ample opportunity to talk, but maintain control of the situation in order to reach the interview objectives. Sometimes it is advisable to let the candidate get off track so they can feel comfortable, and sometimes what they share is enlightening, but always come back to asking for an answer to the original question.

10. Standardize the questions asked—To increase reliability and avoid discrimination, ask the same questions of all applicants for a particular job. Keep careful notes; record facts, impressions, and any relevant information, including what was told to the applicant.

Potential Problems in the Interview

Our goal during an interview is to get accurate and useful information without bias so we can make the best decisions for our departments. We want to ensure that what we believe about a person after an interview is as close to the truth as possible. In essence, we are trying to use the interview to predict the future performance of a candidate. This is difficult, but consistency in comparing apples to apples is critical. Evidence indicates that interviewers make perceptual judgments that are often inaccurate. (Agreement among interviewer's ratings are poor; that is, different conclusions about the applicant.)

> *"Interviewers generally draw early impressions that become very quickly entrenched. If negative information is exposed early in the interview, it tends to be more heavily weighted than if that same information comes out later. Studies indicate that most interviewers' decisions change very little after the first four to five minutes of the interview. As a result, information elicited early in the interview carries greater weight than does information elicited later, and a "good applicant," is probably characterized more by the absence of unfavorable characteristics than by the presence of favorable characteristics."* (Robbins, 128.)

Below are some interviewing pitfalls to be aware of and try to avoid. The goal is to remain unbiased and stay focused throughout the entire interview. Do not pass judgment until the candidate leaves the office. It is also beneficial to ask other's opinions, such as the receptionist, or others who may have had contact with the candidate.

*"During an interview the candidate should talk
and the interviewer should listen."*

Snap Judgments—Some interviewers decide whether an applicant is suitable within the first four to five minutes of the interview and spend the rest of the time looking for evidence to support their judgment. This can also work in the other direction—if an employer really needs someone they may see only what they want to see in an attempt to fill a position with a poorly qualified applicant who isn't a good fit, just because they need a quick fix.

Negative emphasis—When evaluating suitability, unfavorable information about an applicant is often emphasized more than favorable information. This could be related to a leader's tendency toward the Theory X or Theory Y style of management.

Self-Serving Bias—The tendency for individuals to attribute their own successes to internal factors while putting the blame for failures on external factors. Be careful not to disparage other departments, or people. On the flipside, you want to look for the candidate's ability to take responsibility for their own actions. This is how people learn and grow. If they are always blaming others, the likelihood that they will ever see themselves in need of growth or change is very small.

Halo Effect—occurs when an interviewer allows a positive characteristic, such as agreeableness, to overshadow other evidence. For example, if the candidate owns a Dachshund and they mention this in the interview and it just so happens you own a Dachshund and because of this you conclude that, "If they own a Dachshund and I own a Dachshund, then they must be alright. How could someone who has the same taste in dogs as me, be bad?"

Devil's Horn—describes the reverse of the halo effect; this occurs when a negative characteristic, such as inappropriate dress, or poor style, overshadows other traits. For example, the candidate is not into watching television, but because you are a fanatic, you conclude that they must be lost, or that something is wrong with them.

Projection—It's easy to judge others if we assume they're similar to us. For instance, if you want challenge and responsibility in your job, you assume that others want the same. Or, if you're honest and trustworthy, you assume that other people are equally honest and trustworthy. This tendency to attribute one's own characteristics to other people can distort perceptions.

Biases and stereotyping—Similarity bias occurs when interviewers favor or select people that they believe to be like themselves based on a variety of personal factors. Interviewers also should avoid any personal tendencies to stereotype individuals because of demographic characteristics or differences. For instance, age disparities may be a concern as young executives are interviewing more senior personnel. Additionally, applicants' ethnic names and accents can negatively impact personal evaluations, and older workers are sometimes less likely to get interviewed and hired than are younger applicants. This is not only illegal, but you may be missing out on a great employee.

> *"Go into the interview with no preconceived notions. Remember, different than you isn't an indicator or predictor of good or bad performance, it's simply an indication that they may see things differently than you. Embrace diversity and use it for creativity and innovation, not homogenization."*

Types of Questions to Avoid in the Interview Process

These types of questions don't really turn over any rocks, and don't dig into the real person. At the end of the interview you want to feel like you walked into a field full of stones and turned them all over. You want to know as much as possible about the person's potential, past, and present performance. The past is a great predictor of the future. The types of questions below will not allow you to gain insight into the person's potential behavior.

Yes/No Questions—Unless verifying specific information, the interviewer should avoid questions that can be answered with "yes" or "no."

Obvious questions—An obvious question is one for which the interviewer already has the answer and the applicant knows it. This makes the interviewer look unprepared and uneducated.

Questions that rarely produce a true answer—avoid questions that prompt a less-than-honest response. An example is, "how did you get along with co-workers?" The likely answer is, "just fine," but this also presents an opportunity to dig a little deeper.

Leading questions—a leading question is one to which the answer is obvious from the way the question is asked. An example is, "Isn't this area of the country great?" Clearly the interviewer believes it is, so it would be in the candidate's best interest to answer in the affirmative. You could ask the same question without leading the candidate like this, "What do you think about this area of the country?"

Illegal questions—as discussed in the do's and don'ts of interview questions above. Stick to job related questions.

Questions that are not job related—All questions should be directly job related to ensure legality, and to steer clear of bias.

Different Types of Interviews

Structured Interview—an interview that uses a set of standardized questions asked to all applicants. This is important for consistency sake so that each applicant has the opportunity to answer the same questions and hiring managers can compare the answers of the various candidates equally. If consistency is not present, the possibility of a discrimination claim becomes more likely.

Behavioral Interview—applicants are asked to describe how they have performed a certain task or handled a problem in the past, which may predict future actions and show how applicants are best suited for the current job. An example may be, "Tell me about a time when you were able to inspire others to act. How did you do this? What was the outcome?"

Situational Interview—contains questions about how applicants might handle specific job situations. The interviewer typically codes the suitability of the answer, assigns point values, and adds up the total number of points each candidate received.

Non-directive Interview—Uses questions developed from the answers to previous questions. The interviewer asks general questions designed to prompt applicants to describe themselves. The interviewer then uses applicants' responses to shape the next question. The problem with this can be that it is difficult to stay job related, and obtaining comparable data on various applicants. (Mathis, Jackson, 231-232)

In an interview, one would never dismiss the intuition of the interviewer as it relates to their department's needs, but coupling intuition with quantifiable data is critical. If your intuition says, "no," trust it, but it must be verified against the scores from the interview.

Minimum qualifications are paramount, but a good fit is what makes a team. If you have five, seven foot tall centers on a basketball team, your team will likely suffer from lack of quickness, dribbling, and shooting. However, five players who have complementary skills and abilities, like the ability to bring the ball up the court, the ability to shoot well from a distance and quickness to guard the smaller, quicker players on other teams, then you have a competitive team.

The leader needs to analyze their team and determine the areas of weakness, whether it's a better ball handler, rebounder, passer, scorer, shooter and then work to fill those gaps.

> *"You are the team leader, and you need to understand where gaps exist so you can work to close them through the staffing process."*

Chapter 8—Documentation, Investigations, Discipline and Appraisals

A Brief Overview

On the surface, the four dimensions of Leadership and Management this chapter will discuss may seem unrelated. However, the similarity that each of these has with the other is that we must not show **bias,** which is the human tendency to make systematic decisions in certain circumstances based on cognitive factors or an inclination to present or hold a partial perspective at the expense of (possibly equally valid) alternatives. Anything biased generally is one-sided, and therefore lacks a neutral point of view. Bias can come in many forms and is often considered to be synonymous with prejudice (see Chapter 7 for clarification on prejudice) rather than evidence. Secondly, we need to remain **objective,** which is the ability to judge fairly. Objectivity is the opposite of **subjectivity,** which is a person's personal perspective, feelings, beliefs, desires or discovery, as opposed to those made from an independent, objective point-of-view.

These two factors, objectivity and a nonbiased point-of-view are important to the success or failure of Documentation, Investigations, Discipline and Appraisals. If an employee senses that their supervisor may play favorites, or if their supervisor has a world view similar to one employee and not another, the likelihood of bias and subjectivity creeping into these aspects is heightened. If an employee feels that they are not being, "given a fair shake," they will act out accordingly, (refer to expectancy theory and equity theory from Chapter 4 on Motivation for a refresher on these two concepts.)

An employee must know that any investigation which leads to discipline and ultimately an employee's appraisal will be conducted impartially, and that they will be disciplined and evaluated the same as any other similarly situated employee.

> *"An employee's perception of bias or subjectivity*
> *is as real to them as actual bias."*

The outcome of just one employee feeling like they were treated unfairly is sometimes catastrophic to a department or unit. The employee will often spend a majority of their day explaining to everyone else just how wicked their leader is. When this happens, if an employee is not objective and nonbiased themselves it is very easy for a swath of negativity to be cut through the middle of a department. Sides are taken and factions, like a fissure in stone occur.

However, a leader's main objective is to help people grow so they can become better. The investigation, discipline and appraisal process should not be one of conflict or confrontation; it should be viewed as an opportunity to assist an employee that we must assume wants to do what is right.

> *"A leader should help people grow. Take a caring,*
> *compassionate, and concerned attitude when performing an*
> *investigation, discipline or appraisal."*

At the end of an investigation, discipline or appraisal session, the employee should walk away feeling energized, motivated and compelled to do better. Too often leaders look at these aspects of their jobs as something they do not like to perform. The following pages will help leaders gain understanding so that they may view these "unfortunate" aspects of their jobs as an opportunity to help employees grow.

Documentation

The need for documentation is often spawned by a report or complaint from an employee, patient or customer. This then sparks a series of events that must be followed to get to the other side of the investigation smoothly, objectively and accurately. Below are a few housekeeping issues that will allow leaders to navigate the documentation process cleanly.

Desk-File—each leader should have a desk file for each employee they work with. This will allow the leader to make notes, and keep a running total of documented issues that the employee encounters. It is very important that not only negative notes and comments are stored in the desk-file, but positive comments as well. This will help the leader be objective and see an accurate picture of the whole employee, not just the issue at hand. This is often most effective if done via spreadsheet.

Proper Record Keeping in Desk-File—collecting information is critical to the idea of objectivity, however the information you collect must be useful. Useful information about a situation or event contains:

1. Date, time and location of event—as specifically as possible.
2. What was the behavior—describe the situation or problem.
3. Why this behavior was a problem or why was it exceptional.
4. Be diligent with this—nothing is too large or too small to document.
5. Make sure your notes are clear and concise so when you review them later, they make sense.

Also critical to the on-going documentation of employee behavior is that you record observations, comments and terrific performances while using the above criteria. This will help when it comes to appraisal and discipline if necessary and you will have a year's worth of notes to use for the appraisal. This process will also help defend the organization in the event of litigation. Generally though, objective, unbiased, clear and concise documentation practices are the key to avoiding a lawsuit all together.

Investigations

Investigations heighten the sensitivity of employees even when they are not involved, and only act as witnesses. The way a leader handles an investigation can determine the way employees feel toward the leader. If a leader appears to be "out to get someone," employees often ban together to protect the employee under investigation.

Investigations will more often than not take wild twists and turns. During an investigation the pendulum will swing back and forth, and the idea of guilt or innocence will become muddy. This is when we need to dig deeper to understand what exactly happened and why. It isn't uncommon for an employee to report an incident that they have some responsibility for, first, like a child telling on their sibling so that they are heard first and then the other person is put on the defensive. There are always two sides.

"A coin has two sides, but the value is in the middle."

Some practical applications to avoid bias or subjectivity are to follow these simple guidelines.

> **Investigation Guidelines**—these can be used to ensure the process of investigating a complaint will be fair, objective and accurate.
>
> 1. **Determine the Scope**—Identify witnesses, and collect relevant data.
> 2. **Have a Witness Present**—When interviewing employees under investigation, or who are witnesses to an event, always have a non-partial witness present for your protection, and the employees. This also can help validate the notes and conversations you have with the employee.
> 3. **Discretion**—Ask employees to come to your office personally, not over the intercom system or in front of other employees. Ask employees being investigated or witnesses to an event to keep the conversation confidential. Explain to them the importance of this and that they are a very important piece to moving forward.

4. **Leading Questions**—Do not ask leading questions that indicate to the employee or witness the answer you are looking for. Ask open-ended questions like, "Have you witnessed any behavior recently that would cause you to identify a problem or that has caused you concern?" If the employee or witness doesn't respond, only then do you get into the specifics of the incident that is under investigation.

5. **Collect Facts**—We are not interested in opinions, suppositions, or inferences. We want to know what happened and why, not what may have happened or what an employee thought happened.

6. **Document Findings**—Refer to the above section on documentation. Most importantly record the date, time and location of the event.

7. **Review Facts**—Be certain that what has been reported is accurate. Do not let other issues of performance interfere with the situation at hand.

Discipline

Once an employee has been found to have committed some infraction, a leader must handle the current situation the same as other similar situations have been handled. As much as you ask an employee not to talk about their pay, their evaluations, and discipline against them, they do talk about these things. If anything is inconsistent, you have not only jeopardized the trust and respect of employees, but you have also opened the door to discrimination charges. For example, if an employee was terminated for theft, yet another employee wasn't, and the employee that was terminated falls into a protected class (over 40, female, minority, or disabled) as we discussed in the previous chapter, a court will have a hard time understanding why the person in the protected class was terminated while the white, fit, thirty year old man with no disability was not. The only basis for treating one person differently than another is discrimination, which as we learned is directly related to prejudice and bias.

"Discipline is an opportunity to help an employee see the path they need to take for success. Punishment is not the goal."

It isn't uncommon for a leader to avoid disciplinary action for a variety of reasons. As Mathis and Jackson illustrate below, the reasons can vary greatly, but in no sense are these valid reasons not to take disciplinary action with an employee.

"Not taking disciplinary action with an employee is like condoning the behavior. The culture and commitment of other employees will suffer if poor performers are not addressed."

Common Reasons Why Discipline Might Not Be Used

1. **Organizational Culture of Avoiding Discipline**—if the organizational "norm" is to avoid penalizing problem employees, then managers are less likely to use discipline or to terminate problem employees.
2. **Lack of Support**—Many managers do not want to use discipline because they fear that their decisions will not be supported by higher management. The degree of support is also a function of organizational culture.
3. **Guilt**—some managers realize that before they became managers, they committed the same violations as their employees, and therefore do not discipline others for actions they formerly committed.
4. **Fear of Loss of Friendship**—Managers may fear losing friendships or damaging personal relationships if they discipline employees.
5. **Avoidance of Time Loss**—Discipline often requires considerable time and effort. Sometimes it is easier for managers to avoid taking the time required for disciplining, especially if their actions may be overturned on review by higher management.
6. **Fear of Lawsuits**—Managers are increasingly concerned about being sued for disciplining an employee, particularly in regard to the ultimate disciplinary step of termination. (Mathis, Jackson, 529)

Perspectives on Discipline

Discipline is defined as punishment and control gained by obedience or training. The world of work requires a different approach to discipline as new generations unfold and spread their wings to start their careers. To **punish** is to impose a penalty against someone. People are often afraid of punishment and their behavior is curtailed to avoid punishment or harsh outcomes. Remember, as Yoda (the Master Jedi) said in the section on Motivation,

"Fear creates anger, anger creates hatred
and hatred creates suffering."
(Which then leads to increased and often unnecessary turnover.)

We are not interested in blind obedience, or control based on fear or punishment, what we are interested in is commitment to the organizational mission, and people making their own decisions for the right reasons—ideally from a place of intrinsic motivation. Unfortunately, the disciplinary process often leaves the employee feeling as if they were just tied to a post and whipped, as if they were acting in a way to actively undermine the organizational goals. This is normally not the case. Employees have bad days, bad ideas, and sometimes execute those bad ideas on bad days. This doesn't mean they are bad and often the employee feels remorse and does not want to do it again.

"Managers often see discipline as part of changing workers'
behaviors, employees often see discipline as unfair because it
can affect their jobs and careers."(Mathis, Jackson, 528)

Progressive Discipline

The style of discipline that is most prevalent in today's business world is somewhat counterintuitive to the creation of high performing employees. We want employees to grow, and get better, not work in fear of failure or punishment. Remember, a climate of innovation and empowerment comes from the freedom to make decisions and even fail. This process could be called a coaching session to gain commitment, not discipline. Below is the generally accepted concept of discipline—**progressive discipline** which is the use of corrective measures in increasingly more serious steps. Progressive Discipline incorporates steps that become progressively more stringent and are designed to change the employee's inappropriate behavior. (Mathis, Jackson, 530)

Generally, employees feel at odds with their supervisor during the progressive discipline process. This is unnecessary and can lead to poor attitudes, fear, and morale problems. Progressive discipline is common, but not recommended. We need to understand where we have been so we know where we are going.

Stages of Progressive Discipline

Generally, this process takes a four step approach to correcting a person's behavior. It is a step-by-step process that with each infraction takes the employee one step closer to termination. It is scary to the employee and often seems out of his/her control.

Step 1—First Offense—Verbal Warning/Caution—
The employee comes to the leader's office. They sit down. The leader describes the problem and why it is an infraction and asks the employee to sign the verbal warning.

Step 2—Second Offense—Written Warning—
The employee comes to the leader's office. They sit down. The leader describes the problem. Explains it is the second occurrence and that continued issues could result in additional disciplinary action up to and including termination of employment. The leader explains why it is an infraction and asks the employee to sign the warning.

Step 3—Third Offense—Suspension—
The employee comes to the leader's office. They sit down. The leader describes the problem and explains that it is the third occurrence and that continued issues could result in additional disciplinary action up to termination of

employment. They explain why it is an infraction and ask the employee to sign the suspension form.

Step 4—Fourth Offense—Termination—

The employee comes to the leader's office. They sit down. The leader describes the problem, and that because this is the fourth time, it has led to termination of employment.

Positive or Non-Punitive Discipline

Positive or non-punitive discipline is very different from progressive discipline. Positive discipline requires employees to take responsibility for their actions. It requires employees to evaluate themselves and decide if they can make a commitment to change their behavior or not. **Positive discipline** is defined as a system of discipline that focuses on the early correction of employee misconduct, with the employee taking total responsibility for correcting the issue. Of course the leader will act as a resource for the employee through the process, but at all times holds the employee fully responsible for their own behavior. The key to a successful positive discipline process is that employees have a clear understanding as to what is expected of them. Just as we will learn in the appraisal process, you can't criticize an employee or discipline them if they are not clear as to what is expected of them. Often leaders assume that employees should understand what expectations are but, as we know, many organizations do things differently and to compound this each leader has different expectations. There are still four steps, but the process is very different.

> *"It is better for an employee to not want to disappoint their leader, rather than fear them. The difference between progressive and positive discipline is fear and disappointment in the."*

Positive Discipline—Attendance Issue

Step 1 - You would let the employee know that they are approaching their limit for absences. You may say something like, "Hey, I just wanted to let you know that you only have two more unscheduled absences left and we have three more months in the reporting period. Were you aware of this? (Of course, they will say, "Yes.") Good, your co-workers and I need you here at work for the success of our team. You are valuable to the success of our team. When someone is absent I'm sure you know how it can affect the entire staff's day. Can you commit to staying under the absenteeism limit?" The employee will respond with "Yes," committing to do this. The ball is now in their court.

Step 2 - If absences continue, you may ask them to recommit to addressing this problem. This time you are going to ask for their commitment in writing. You will use the guidelines for documenting employee behavior and ask for their commitment again to correct the problem. Say something to them in a written statement such as "the organization needs your commitment to meet our absenteeism standards. We agreed upon the terms of employment at the time you were hired and you need to adhere to these commitments." Leave a space for the employee to sign, acknowledging this commitment. It becomes an informal contract. The employee doesn't want to break their word by failing to meet his or her commitment and if they do, it is their decision and they know the consequences.

Step 3 - And of course occasionally an employee will break their commitment and the attendance problems will resurface. This time the leader will address the issue with a written statement detailing what has happened to this point. The statement will include that the employee has made two prior commitments and failed to honor these commitments of employment and is being asked to take a day off **with or without pay** (let them use PTO time if they want.) They need to decide whether or not this is a behavior that can be immediately corrected or if they need to resign their employment with the organization. The employee will bring the statement back to work the next day and sign it if he or she can make the commitment or resign if they feel they cannot. It is their decision.

Step 4 - If the employee commits to correcting the behavior by signing the statement and the problem persists, then you will be forced to make an employment decision for the employee. Still, there will be no surprises.

Appraisals

"There should be no surprises in the appraisal process."

Performance appraisals are intended to measure how well an employee is meeting job requirements. However, performance appraisals often don't measure this at all. Sometimes they measure how popular an employee is with the leader, or how well the employee has done in the last month, and sometimes they are even measured against other employees rather than against what the job description warrants. Employees can be blind-sided by poor performance on their appraisal. This should never happen. Employees should know what they are to do and leaders should address problem areas so that the employee doesn't think the behavior is o.k. As we discussed in the Ethics and Recognition chapter, they should also be told about the positive aspects as they occur. There should be no surprises in the evaluation process—good or bad. Remember, employees crave feedback, they want to do well, and it is the leader's job to ensure the employee is aware how their performance is being viewed by their leader.

Appraisal Guidelines

1. Performance ratings must be job related.
2. Employees must be given a written copy of their job standards in advance of appraisals and, ideally, at the time of hire.
3. Leaders who conduct the appraisal must be able to observe the behavior they are rating. This implies having a measurable standard with which to evaluate employee behavior.
4. Leaders must be trained to use the appraisal form correctly. They should be instructed in how to apply appraisal standards when making judgments.
5. Appraisals should be discussed openly with the employees and counseling or corrective guidance offered to help poor performers improve performance.
6. An appeal procedure should be established to enable employees to express disagreement with the appraisal. (Bohlander, Snell)

Potential Pitfalls to Successful and Positive Appraisals

Of course, too often there are surprises and the appraisal process turns into a negative experience for both the leader and employee very quickly. Employees should know what to expect at appraisal time. They should be in contact with their leaders so they are aware of improvement areas prior to being evaluated on those areas. It is unrealistic for an employee to improve performance if they are unaware that performance is suffering. Address issues as they arise and let the employee know what it was about their performance that was substandard and what they can do to improve their performance in a given area.

Reasons Appraisals Sometimes Fail

1. Managers feel that little or no benefit will be derived from the time and energy spent in the process.
2. Managers dislike the face-to-face confrontation of appraisal interviews.
3. Managers are not sufficiently adept in providing appraisal feedback.
4. The judgmental role of appraisal conflicts with the helping role of developing employees. (Bohlander, Snell)

Performance Appraisals—Rater Errors

Similar to interviewing and the biases that may impede a positive hiring decision, there are many different types of appraisal errors. Each of them can lead to trouble when one or more fall into the employee's appraisal. An employee has a preconceived notion as to what the job duties are but, more accurately, they should be working from a correct and accurate job description because the job description is the basis for performance review. Often these preconceived notions are inaccurate or the proper way to perform a job has not been detailed to the employee, but that is a training issue. When an employee feels they are performing one way and then their performance evaluation says otherwise, they feel discontented, disheartened and frustrated. There are many rater errors that can affect performance appraisals and it is important to understand and be able to identify them and, more importantly, avoid them all together. Is it possible to avoid them all together? Yes . . . but you must have the knowledge, understanding and commitment to do so. These will look familiar to you, but it is important to reiterate the value in avoiding these errors.

Halo Error—occurs when the employee performs outstanding in one area and because of this all other areas are rated outstanding. This could be from focusing too much attention on one aspect of the job and neglecting the rest. For example, if everyone likes the employee and their interpersonal skills are outstanding but their work is below average and the leader rates them high in all areas because they are so well liked, this error has occurred. It is not fair or appropriate to the employee or co-workers if all aspects of employment are not validly and accurately appraised.

Horn Error—occurs the opposite of the halo error in that if one area is poor all areas will be rated poorly.

Error of Central Tendency—is when the appraiser rates all or most of the employees being appraised around the mid-point of the pay scale. This could occur because the supervisor is afraid to hurt feelings or cause problems. But what this does is de-motivates people to work hard.

> *"The effect of central tendency is to*
> *de-motivate people to work hard."*

The supervisor or appraiser is not doing the employee or the organization any favors by evaluating everyone as mediocre. They are actually doing a disservice to both. Employees do not know how they are truly doing so there is no motivation to improve. The status quo has been set and you can expect even the good employees to fall to mediocrity.

Leniency or Strictness Error—is when the appraiser scores the employees unusually high or low. Again, the reasoning for this is similar to the error of central tendency. Managers, supervisors and appraisers are either afraid to hurt feelings and score everyone at a higher level than they should, hoping to gain popularity or they feel that no person is perfect and there is always room for improvement. Of course we have to remember that we are working from job descriptions and if an employee far exceeds one aspect of the job description, their evaluation should reflect that excellence.

Recency Error—is when an employee is rated on recent behavior rather than for the entire appraisal period. For example, if an employee has been producing an incredible amount of work for the last quarter, but has failed to meet standards for the prior three quarters, under this error they may receive an outstanding rating. This is an error.

> *"The evaluation period is for the entire year,*
> *not just the last quarter."*

Contrast Error—occurs when an employee is rated either higher or lower based on the previous employees rating being either high or low. Under this error, you certainly do not want to be rated after the superstar, especially if you are just meeting standards.

> *"Each employee should be rated based on their job description,*
> *not on how they compare to other employees."*

Similar-to-me-Error—occurs when the rater evaluates the employee and inflates the rating based on some mutual personal connection. For example, an employee is appraised incredibly high, because the appraiser and the employee share some common interest such as sailing. This error is common when there is favoritism or nepotism.

These errors occur naturally in people because we do judge and come to conclusions without knowing all the facts. The key to avoiding these errors and rating employees on the merit of their performance is to understand the errors, decide you will not let them into the appraisal and work to avoid them.

Appraisal Checklist

Use the checklist below to ensure you are properly executing the performance appraisal and doing what you can to enable the process to be positive.

"The appraisal process should be a positive experience for the leader and the employee."

Scheduling

1. Schedule the review and notify the employee ten to fourteen days in advance.
2. Ask the employee to prepare for the session by reviewing his or her performance, job objectives, and development goals.
3. Clearly state that this will be a formal, annual performance appraisal.

Preparing for the Appraisal

1. Review the performance documentation collected throughout the year in your desk file. Concentrate on work patterns that have developed.
2. Be prepared to give specific examples of above, or below-average performance.
3. When performance falls short of expectations, determine what changes need to be made. If performance meets or exceeds expectations, discuss this and plan how to reinforce it.
4. After the appraisal is written, set it aside for a few days and then review it again.

Conducting a Positive Appraisal

1. Select a location that is comfortable and free of distractions. The location should encourage a frank and candid conversation. It is not advisable for the leader to sit behind a desk while the employee sits in front of them. Find a neutral space.

2. Discuss each topic in the appraisal one at a time, consider strengths and short comings.
3. Be specific and descriptive, not general and judgmental. Report occurrences rather than judging them.
4. Discuss your differences and resolve them. Solicit agreement with the evaluation.
5. Jointly discuss and design plans for taking corrective action for growth and development.
6. Maintain a professional and supportive approach to the appraisal discussion.

Benefits of Proper Appraisal

Allowing rater errors to slip into evaluations could result in a discrimination charge. Training managers to understand rater errors and avoid them will help maintain the unbiased appraisals that lead to success. A biased appraisal will lead to lack of employee motivation and drag everyone to mediocrity. If employees are not evaluated accurately it causes them to feel as if their hard work is for nothing. The reward must match the effort. This inspires effort and improvement. Remember the Chapter on Motivation, expectancy theory states the effort put forth must match the reward offered. If the reward is less than the effort required to obtain the reward, motivation will be low.

Employees and the organization benefit when employees are treated fairly, unbiased and recognized for their effort accurately. When employees are accurately evaluated they are given the opportunity to improve and feel appreciated for their efforts. Ambiguity is diminished and you as their leader have given the employee the tools to succeed and feel good about it once they have improved.

Leadership Distilled—The 8 Elements of Leadership

We have discussed eight simple ideas for effective leadership. These ideas should be used as guideposts when you become uncertain how to deal with an employee or situation. The more you refer to them, the more likely they will become who you are as a leader, and as a person. Remember, you can be as good as you want to be. The tools are available, but you must use them consistently and often. <u>Rip the following page out and post it so you can refer to it often.</u>

Shine!—8 Elements of Leadership

#1—*"Different is not better or worse."*

#2—*"Stop talking and listen."*

#3—*"Leadership is like water. Management is like stone."*

#4—*"We must 'Answer the Why.'"*

#5—*"Invest time, energy and effort at the front-end of change."*

#6—*"Recognize employees for behaviors you want to encourage."*

#7—*"Hire hard so you can manage easy."*

#8—*"A coin has two sides, but the value is in the middle."*

"It is up to you as to how you want to be followed!"

Bibliography

Borchert, M. Donald, Stewart, David II, *Exploring Ethics,* MacMillan Publishing Company, 1986

Daft, L. Richard, Marcic, Dorothy, *Understanding Management,* Harcourt College Publishers, 3rd edition, 2001

Robbins, P. Stevens, *Organizational Behavior,* 10th Edition, Prentice Hall, 2003

Bateman, S. Thomas, Snell A. Scott, *Management, Competing in the New Era,* McGraw-Hill Irwin, 5th edition, 2002

Bohlander, George and Snell, Scott. *Managing Human Resources,* Thomson, Southwestern 13th Edition, 2004

French, Wendell, Human Resources Management, Houghton Mifflin Publishers, 4th Edition, 1998

Lesiker, Raymond.V., Flately, Marie, E., *Basic Business Communication, Skills for Empowering the Internet Generation, 2002*

Guffey, E. Mary, *Essentials of Business Communication,* Thomas, Southwestern, 6th Edition, 2004

Myers, Gail E., Myers, Michelle Tolela, *The Dynamics of Human Communication: A Laboratory Approach,* McGraw-Hill, 6th Edition, 1992

Northouse, G. Peter, *Leadership, Theory and Practice,* Sage Publications, Inc., 2nd Edition, 2001

Kouzes M. James, Posner, Z. Barry, *The Leadership Challenge*, Jossey-Bass, 1997.

Myers, G. David *Psychology,* Worth Publishers, 3rd Edition, 1992

French, L. Wendell, Bell, H. Cecil Jr, *Organizational Development, Behavior Science Interventions for Organization Improvement,* 5th Edition, Prentice Hall, 1995.

Mathis, L. Robert, Jackson, H. John, *Human Resources Management,* 13th Edition, South Western Cengage Learning, 2011

Merriam Webster, *Websters Ninth New Collegiate Dictionary*, 1988.

Heneman, Herbert, G. III, Heneman, Robert, L. Judge, Timothy, A. *Staffing Organizations*, 2nd Edition, The Mcgraw-Hill Company, Inc. 1997

Internet Sources

http://www.ted.com/talks/lang/en/amy_cuddy_your_body_language_shapes_who_you_are.html

http://www.ted.com/talks/margaret_heffernan_dare_to_disagree.html

http://www.ted.com/talks/lang/en/barry_schwartz_on_our_loss_of_wisdom.html

http://www.ted.com/talks/lang/en/drew_dudley_everyday_leadership.html

http://www.ted.com/talks/simon_sinek_how_great_leaders_inspire_action.html?source=email#.T5Wc3b4ulWh.email

http://www.ted.com/talks/lang/en/shawn_achor_the_happy_secret_to_better_work.html

http://thegroundfloor.typepad.com

Made in the USA
Lexington, KY
30 October 2017